No Love Lost

A comedy

Rony Robinson

Samuel French — London
New York   Toronto   Hollywood

Rights of Performance by Amateurs are controlled by Samuel French Ltd, 52 Fitzroy Street, London W1P 6JR, and they, or their authorized agents, issue licences to amateurs on payment of a fee. **It is an infringement of the Copyright to give any performance or public reading of the play before the fee has been paid and the licence issued.**

The Royalty Fee indicated below is subject to contract and subject to variation at the sole discretion of Samuel French Ltd.

> Basic fee for each and every
> performance by amateurs   Code M
> in the British Isles

The Professional Rights in this play are controlled by Peters Fraser and Dunlop Ltd, 503/4 The Chambers, Chelsea Harbour, London, SW10 OXF

ISBN 0 573 01810 3

Please see page iv for further copyright information

CHARACTERS

Max Johnson, a historian
Kate, Max's departing wife
Anna, their elder daughter
Emma, their younger daughter
Jenny, Kate's mother
Daniel, Kate's father
Noon, an alternative therapist
Jeff, a man from the motor trade
Frank, a shop assistant

The action of the play takes place in Max's sitting-room
and Kate's sitting-room

Time: ACT I: June back to last Christmas
        ACT II: Last Christmas forward to June

SYNOPSIS OF SCENES

ACT I   Max's Sitting-Room

PROLOGUE

SCENE 1   Late on a late June evening

SCENE 2   Three weeks earlier, a Sunday morning in May

SCENE 3   Five weeks earlier, a Friday morning in April

SCENE 4   Three weeks earlier, a Friday evening in March

SCENE 5   A fortnight earlier, an early evening in March

SCENE 6   Three weeks earlier, a Saturday afternoon in late February

SCENE 7   A fortnight earlier, a Sunday morning in mid February

SCENE 8   Six weeks earlier, late afternoon, right at the end of Christmas

ACT II   Kate's Sitting-Room

SCENE 1   Late last December

SCENE 2   Six weeks later, an evening in mid February

SCENE 3   A few days later, a Saturday morning in February

SCENE 4   A few weeks later, a March evening

SCENE 5   A few days later, that Friday in early March

SCENE 6   Next morning, very early on a Saturday in March

SCENE 7   Several weeks later, a Sunday morning in May

SCENE 8   A fortnight later, Sunday afternoon in June

EPILOGUE

NO LOVE LOST

No Love Lost was written for the BT Biennial 1998 and performed all over Great Britain by drama groups, in various ways, during a fortnight in October 1998.

The author was the co-director of one of the first productions and he has appended Production Notes to the text which can be found on page 81.

For Eleanor Robinson Thom

ACKNOWLEDGEMENT

Extracts from *When We Are Married* by J B Priestley are quoted by kind permission of Peters Fraser and Dunlop on behalf of the Estate of J B Priestley.

ACT I

PROLOGUE

It is a few minutes before the show proper begins

Late in the June evening of Max's retirement. The Lighting on stage is fairly dim, the auditorium Lights are still on, and some of the audience are still arriving

Everyone apart from Kate is waiting for Max to return and be surprised by a secret party. They mingle, pleasantly talking, joking, drinking; we can't hear most of what they say because party music is playing

They take no notice of the audience and the audience doesn't take much notice of them

When they get the word from the stage manager that the play proper is starting, Emma at the window sees Max coming. She warns the others

Anna cuts the music

Frank is told to switch the light off, which he does

Everyone hides

This prologue can be left out. If it is, this is where the play really begins

SCENE 1

Max's sitting-room. Late on a late June evening

The room is in darkness

We hear Max at his door not finding it easy to get in

Max (*off*) Here we are.

We hear Max struggling

> Home at last.

Max comes into his dark sitting-room. He tries to turn on the Lights

> Light switch on. Light not on.
> Light switch on. Light not on again.
> One more go for luck. Light switch on. Light not on.

Anna shines her torch in Max's face and sings "Happy Birthday" to her Daddy

Max I don't suppose, Anna, my beautiful daughter, that you know where I keep my spare light bulbs?

Anna I know a joke about how many men it takes to *change* a light bulb.

Max One of your mother's jokes, if I remember?

Anna You remember too much.

Max Historians have to remember too much.

Anna Are you OK, Dad?

Max Sherry tonight.
> A difficult drink. It can't quite make up its mind what it's supposed to do to you.

Anna I hope it's not done too much.
> Because we've taken the bulb out!
> Because!
> For you!
> Max Johnson!
> On your birthday and the day of your early retirement.
> Surprise surprise!

Max It is a bit.

Anna Max Johnson? Do you remember this voice?

Jeff (*hidden*) I've got you this nice green Renault Espace RN/Helios? Very French, very stylish? Thirteen grand?

Jeff comes out and turns the Lights on

Anna Yes, all the way from the *Plume of Feathers*! Your old pal—Jeff!

Jeff Your round, mate!

Max Jeff!

Jeff gives Max a drink

Jeff Cheers!

Jenny (*hidden*) Well, I'm really sorry but I've spent quite long enough
   crunched up here with him.
   (*She pops up*) Give us a kiss and let's get it over with.
Anna Yes, it's the voice of your very own mother-in-law!
Jenny He *did* kiss me once. I don't suppose he remembers.
Max I have to remember. I'm a historian. (*He kisses Jenny*)
Anna And next!
   Back together *with* Grans after their recent troubles!
   Her dear husband Daniel, formerly known as *Gramps*!

Daniel pops up

Daniel Right, well, I'm ready for it!
Jenny He was never ready for anything.
Daniel I thought we'd agreed to stop complaining about me.
Jenny I'd never agree to that.

Daniel shakes Max's hand

Anna Max Johnson, do your recognize this voice?

There is no voice

   This voice!

Anna reveals Emma

   Your younger daughter, the very wonderful and very silent—Emma!

Emma doesn't speak and is cuddled by Jenny

Max Em?
   You look … very wonderful.
   Right, well, if there's no-one else?
Anna There is!
   A woman who knows more about you than most!
   Do you recognize *this* voice?
Noon (*hiding*) Hi, Max!
Anna A bit louder?
Jenny It's not the right woman.
Noon Hi, Max!
Max (*not pleased*) Noon?
Jenny It should be his *wife*.

Noon (*emerging*) Hi!
Max Hi again.
　　　Jeff, this is Noon, my therapist.
Jeff I know.
Noon Hi!

Noon and Jeff hug

Max Eh?
Jeff Noon cured my shoulder.
Max She tried to cure me.
Jeff Too much lifting the elbow I'm afraid.
Noon Don't be afraid, Jeff.
　　　We don't have to be afraid!
Max Good, well, who else needs introducing?
　　　Noon—this is Gramps.
Noon We've met, haven't we, Daniel?
Max How can you have?
Jenny She was round Kate's that afternoon.
Max What afternoon?
Daniel That funny afternoon.
Jenny When he cried.
Daniel Didn't cry.
Jenny And said he loved me.
Daniel Didn't say I loved you.
Jenny And begged me to have him back.
Daniel Didn't beg.
Jenny You begged.
Daniel And I weren't really crying.
Jenny *Wasn't* really crying.
Daniel Exactly.
Noon We were all crying.
Max I've got a feeling I missed something?

During the following, Frank pops out unnoticed with flowers

Noon Oh, you did, Max.
　　　We were round Kate's.
　　　And everything—*moved*!
Anna Frank—I'd forgotten you.
Frank I do get forgotten.
Anna Diddums.
Frank For you this time, Mr Johnson.

Max Thanks! (*He takes the flowers*)
Jenny Kate should be here.
It's like funerals. When you don't do them right, people don't believe
you're dead, and then where are you?
Daniel Dead.
Jenny Exactly.
Jeff To Max!
A long early retirement and may all his troubles be little ones!
All Max!
Jeff (*leading everyone in*) For he's a jolly good fellow
All For he's a jolly good fellow
For he's a jolly good fellow
And so say all of us.
And so say all of us
And so say all of us
For he's a jolly good fellow
And so say all of us!
Jeff Speech!
Max You don't want a speech!
Anna Do Rasputin, Dad.

They react with enthusiasm

Max You don't want Rasputin!
Anna We do!
Anyone not want Rasputin?
Anyone not *heard* Rasputin?

Only Frank's hand goes up

Max *You* should have heard Rasputin?
Frank He was when I had my adenoids, sir.
Jenny Have a toffee.
Frank No, thank you very much.
The last one you gave me pulled out my filling.
Anna Take your seats please, everyone!
The historian Mr Max Johnson will now once again attempt his party
piece!
His emergency lesson throughout his long teaching career, ending
today!
The Extraordinary Death of Rasputin!
And as usual we are all the revolting peoples of all the
Russias, *and* all his sound effects!

Applause!

They applaud

Max Thank you for coming everyone.
I'm sorry I was late.
Lovely surprise though—Anna.
Jeff.
Noon.
Grans.
Gramps.
Emma.
Oh, and Frank of course. Nearly forgot him.
Frank People do forget me, Mr Johnson.
Anna Diddums.
Max Rasputin you want, right?
Right.
Imagine then, first, a dark night in Moscow, with a Siberian wind blowing through the long corridors of the Imperial Palace.

Everyone has to listen carefully. Max never tells the death of Rasputin the same way. Anna encourages participation in the sound effects, including Emma using her instrument

Deep inside the Kremlin, Czar Nicholas himself waits shivering!

Sound effects

Even he can feel the cold breath of history!

Sound effects

Outside beyond the thick Imperial curtains, there falls a soft Russian snow!

Sound effects

Listen now to the sandalled feet of a strange priest padding up and down the Siberian cold corridors outside his door!

Sound effects

And hear, mumbling to himself and chewing his long beard——

Sound effects

> The mad monk who cannot die!
> *Rasputin!*

The phone rings

> Don't answer it.
> Everyone I care about is already in this room.
> **Frank** That's a really nice thing to say, Mr Johnson.
> **Jenny** It's not a really nice thing to say in front of his real wife's mother.

Jeff lifts the receiver

Max Rasputin!

They listen, and find it comical

Jeff (*on the phone*) Moscow in the deepest mid winter?
> I sound funny because I'm not Max...
> I would have come to see it but my BMW blew up on the motorway and...
> He's just started doing his talk about Rasput...
> (*To Max*) Kate.

Max takes the phone

Max Hallo?

The Lights flicker

> (*To the audience*) Why?
> And why now?
> Six months after she left me?
> We *historians* of course know that the only way we can ever make sense of things is to look at them backwards.
> When *we* know what came next.

The party-goers exit

> (*To the audience*) So going backwards...
> To three weeks *before* the big surprise party.
> On a Sunday morning in May.

When *Gramps* has already been living with me for several weeks.
Grans suddenly turns up, with his stuff.
And this is three weeks earlier, remember.

SCENE 2

Three weeks earlier. A Sunday morning in May

Emma is playing her instrument in her room

Jenny pokes in with her bags

Max Thank goodness! (*He kisses her*)
Jenny You've never kissed me on purpose before.
       Being a widow must suit me.
Max You're not a widow, Jenny.
Jenny People are more impressed by widows.
Max Your husband is alive and well, up in my shed.
Jenny These are his deceased effects. (*She hands over one bag of things*)
Max I kept on ringing you, but you're never at home.
Jenny And I never will be now, will I?
       (*She indicates Emma's playing*) Emma still holding you hostage?
Max Go and ask her while I go up to the shed and tell him you're here.
Jenny I won't be if you do.
Max We can all have a cup of tea.
Jenny Have you drunk *his* tea?
Max Yes.
Jenny I think that's all that needs to be said, then.
Max You married him. For better or worse?
Jenny I never knew how worse it was going to get.
       I've rejoined the C of E, dear. I must say they are very good with new
       widows.
       My vicar says we are on earth to fulfil ourselves.
       Well, as I told you privately, and I've told the vicar and the curate too,
       I have not been fulfilled for nine years by anybody's counting.
Max Gramps. Can't. Go. On. Staying At My House.
Jenny Sorry, dear?
Max He. Has. To. Go. Home. To. Your. House.
Jenny I. Have. Not. Got. A. House.
       I've sold his house for far less than it was worth.

Emma's music stops

Just as I have sold his car for far less than that was worth.

Max Gramps is your husband.

Jenny And Kate is your *wife*.

Max She *left* me.

Jenny *He* left me.

Max And came to live with me.

Jenny And now I'm leaving him.

Max My wife runs off, so your husband comes to live with me!

Jenny You started it.

Max You can't just *leave* him here?

Jenny I didn't just *bring* him here, did I?

Max And what about your "stickability"?

Jenny You and Kate set us a very good example of my "stickability".
You've wrecked everybody's lives just so you could be happy.
Well, you're *not* going to be.
(*She hands over the medicines as she identifies them*) Athlete's foot
cream, mornings.
Ditto toenail fungus tincture.
Don't interrupt, dear, I'm not going to be kept talking until he turns up
again.
TCP.
Smokers Tooth Powder.
Zambuk.
Lung tonic.
All out of date.
Goodbye for ever.

Max What shall I tell him?

Jenny Tell him that neither the athlete's foot cream nor the toenail fungus
tincture can be expected to work without persistent application.
And when he tells you he can't reach his own feet, tell him you'll do
them for him.

Max I can't do——

Jenny (*fiercely*) No, but you could give him asylum when he ran away from
me, couldn't you?
And you can sit up with him all night long talking about football while
I slowly turn into a widow?
Can't you?
And you neither of you know the first thing about football, do you?
Well, goodbye men, say I. (*And she really is going*)

Max Have you told Kate?

Jenny Important rule learned over the years.
If you want to do anything that includes Kate, don't tell her.

Max *She* must have Gramps.

Jenny Not in the circumstances.

Jenny goes out

Max What circumstances?
Jenny (*off*) And tell him *a wife's not just for Christmas.*

The door slams

Max turns back in to find Daniel watching

Daniel Impressive woman.
        From a distance.
Max You were there all the time?
Daniel Thanks to your solidarity, Max, I'm always here all the time now.

The Lights flicker

Max (*to the audience*) Gramps wasn't *always* here all the time.
        Nothing is for always. Ask any historian.
        But you are asking why is he here *now*?
        What was the *occasion* and the *cause*?
        The long term *circumstances* and the short term *reason*?
        Good! These are the questions we historians must ask.
        So—ever backwards!
        Five weeks *earlier*.
        Twenty past six, and we're having early morning tea with Gramps as
        if he has always been here, and always means to be.

SCENE 3

Five weeks earlier. A Friday morning in April

Anna and Max slump

Daniel enters with a tray of tea things

Daniel I've made her tea every morning of our marriage and she never once
        said anything good about it.
        Too hot.
        Too much milk.
        The wrong sort of milk.

Too much tea.
After the first ten years I did it wrong on purpose to see if she'd notice the difference.
She didn't.
Even when I used my own bathwater.
Imagine starting every day with her telling you off?

Max reaches out for the tea. Daniel pushes him

Tea's like life. Put good things in, and take your time. It'll all come round. (*He moves away from Max, taking the tea with him*)
Your dad's a hero, Emma.
Anna Anna.
Daniel He's the explorer who shows the way for the rest of us.
He's the Captain Scott of modern marriage.
Appreciate that, do you?
Anna Not sure what you're on about actually, Gramps.
Daniel Captain Scott!
Anna Who?
Daniel Explored the Arctic.
Anna Why?
Daniel And died.
Anna Oh.
Daniel Then there's Captain Webb.
Anna What did he do?
Daniel He *didn't* die. Well, he did, course, but not straight away.
Know what he did, do you?
Anna No.
Daniel Swam the channel.
Ended up in a matchbox.
He's history, like me and your dad like.
You, you're too young. You've missed everything.
Anna Have you been drinking, Gramps?
Daniel No, and I'll never need to drink again.
And I never thought I'd live long enough to hear myself say *that*. (*He fusses with the tea*)
Anna What does Grans say about you leaving her?
Daniel Nothing.
Anna Doesn't sound like her.

Emma enters, unseen, in her pyjamas to continue sleeping

Daniel She's still asleep.

No-one's brought her early morning tea yet, you see. And *never will again*!

Max reaches for the tea. Daniel slaps him

Tea's like life. Put good things in and take your time. It'll all come round.
And *she* wants to speak up for herself.

Anna She's not "spoken up for herself" for three months.

Daniel I'll speak up for her, then.
One last burst of autumn colour before the winter that's coming for ever.
I've heard them down the club. When they lose their wives and husbands, they can't stop talking. Any old stuff gushing out everywhere. Then course the next thing they're saying everything twice, and they can't remember if they've had their own breakfast. (*He wonders*)
I haven't, have I?

Max reaches out for the tea. Daniel smacks him with a spoon

I'll stay in your shed all day.
And I'll cook you your suppers?
Proper pork suppers?

Anna We're vegetarian.

Max Not.

Anna You *are*.

Max Not any more.

Anna So just because Mum's gone, it's OK to eat dead bodies now?
To execute and drown and gas millions of millions of our fellow creatures every day? To build concentration camps for chickens on every farm in——

Max Tell your *mother*.

Anna *Mother* told *us*.

Max Mother told us a lot of things.

Daniel Shall *I* be mother? (*He at last pours the tea*)
And I'll tell you why I love history.
Everybody's dead in history.
You get a bit of peace in history.
Oh yes, we'll have some nice little chats about history.

Anna He'll be able to tell you Rasputin every night. *For ever.*

Daniel I'm good at being told.
I've made her tea every morning of our marriage and she never once said anything good about it.

Too hot.
Too much milk.
The wrong sort of milk.
Too much tea. (*He passes the tea*)

Anna and Max take it. Emma is asleep

After the first ten years I did it wrong on purpose, see if she'd notice
the difference.
She didn't.
Even when I made it with my own bathwater.
Imagine starting every day with her telling you off.
Have I just said that?
Anna Yes.

Max drinks. Anna drinks. The tea isn't good

Max What did Grans say about your tea?
Daniel Too hot. Too much milk. The wrong sort of milk. Too much tea.
Max Historic moment coming up.
A first.
I *agree with Grans.*
Your tea is utterly undrinkable.
Never make it again!

Long gloomy pause

Daniel I can stay though, can't I?
Please?

They don't say no

Thanks.
Only I daren't go back to her now.
Thanks.
Cheers. (*He tastes his own tea, which is horrible, but he has to drink it*)

Max turns to the audience

The Lights flicker

Max (*to the audience*) Captain Webb?
Captain Scott?

There are so many people in history who were nothing like as interesting as they thought they were.

Max Johnson's first rule of history... You only know if you *really* matter after you're dead.

Daniel and Anna go

There is an assertive knocking at the door

Three weeks *earlier.*
A cool evening in March.
And Grans is calling with a banana.

SCENE 4

Three weeks earlier. An evening in March

Max goes out

We hear the noisy arrival of Jenny, off

Jenny (*off*) No kiss, dear?
Max (*off*) No thanks, Grans.
          Hallo, sweetheart. Kiss?
          No, all right.
Jenny Not all right at all.
          Stickability is what some people need.
          Her grandfather's infinitely worse but I stayed stuck.

Jenny sweeps in with bananas

Emma follows with the last bits of a burger meal, and her musical instrument

She sits, with her feet up whenever Jenny doesn't notice

          I'm not going into it here and now. But I've never been able to explain her grandfather and the towels. (*She is already tidying up*) You realize she's been gone three months?
Max So?
Jenny So it's time we got her back before she gets used to it.
          You worked out why she went in the first place, yet?

Max She got fed up with me.

Jenny She was always "fed up" with you.

Max She'd always got the *causes*. But she had to wait for the *occasion*.
It is the vital difference we need to understand if we are ever to
understand history at all.
Take, for example, the familiar question "What caused the First World
War?"
The familiar answer is "The Archduke Franz Ferdinand got shot".
Well, yes. He was the *occasion*.
But was he the *cause* or causes?

Jenny (*very sharply*) Stickability. Not history.

Max No.

Jenny Yes.
I've just been round to see her.
Off out.
Some play in Manchester.*
With a man.
Going off out never solves anything.

Max I go off out. Sometimes.

Jenny *You always have to come back.*
I now want to see you eat this banana.
You never did eat properly in this house.
Luckily, I've got two beef casseroles in the car.
Gramps and I haven't had what our doctor recognizes as a full married
life for nine years.

Emma is interested

You knew that, of course?

Max No.

Jenny Then what on earth do you talk with him about on those long walks
at Christmas?

Max Football.

Jenny He's not been to a football match since we were married.

Max Nor me.

Jenny You silly men.
You just switch off the light and hope for the best, don't you?
We never had bananas. You don't remember the war, of course.

Max Of course I do. I'm a historian so I have to remember everything.

Jenny In which case perhaps you can remember the married life side of *your*
married life then?

---

* Or similar suitable location not too far away where people do plays and stay up after
10 o'clock at night.

Emma is more interested

Max If you mean what I think you mean, it wasn't too bad.
Jenny How not too bad?
Max Better than the, er, *unmarried* side anyway.

They notice Emma's interest

Jenny Come and tell me while you get the casseroles from the car.
    Unless you'd prefer me to rupture myself, of course?

 Jenny leaves

Max On balance, I think I'd prefer you to rup——
Jenny (*off*) I'll *make her come back to you.*

 Max turns to see Emma leaving

Max Emma. Talk?

The Lights flicker

    Max Johnson's second and third rules of history.
    Two: even people in the past didn't know what was coming next even
    if we do now and…
    Three: it didn't feel like the past when it was.
    Thus, a fortnight even *earlier.*
    An evening in March
    I've gone off out myself.
    Then I've come back in again.

 Max goes

SCENE 5

A fortnight earlier. An early evening in March

Jeff comes into the empty room

Unsurely, he susses out the drinks and helps himself

Max comes in

Jeff   All right, mate, I just...?
Max   Fine, yes.
          Good of you to come round, Jeff.
Jeff   Got your message, mate.
          Nice place.
Max   You saying that to try to get me to buy a motor?
Jeff   Funny that. I got a nice little...
          No—your door was wide open.
Max   That'll be Gramps.
Jeff   Who's "Gramps" when he's at home?
Max   He's not at home.
          He's Kate's father.
Jeff   That old feller sitting on the wall?
Max   That'll be him.
Jeff   I've got him very interested in a little Proton Persona one-point-three
          GLi Compact hatchback I might just be able to get hold of.
          I think he's been drinking.
Max   My Drambuie from Christmas!
Jeff   He wanted to talk about football.
Max   He does.
Jeff   I think he mistook me for that football bloke on the telly all the women
          fancy.
          Reasonable mistake, eh?
          Trouble is, mate, I don't know anything about football.
Max   Nor him.
Jeff   So—we got your message, down at the *Plume*?
Max   Right. Good.
Jeff   You've not been down the *Plume*?
Max   I usually stay in these days.
Jeff   Why's that, then?
Max   Kate's left me.
Jeff   Right.
          Down the *Plume* we thought it might be serious.
          In fact, we concluded you'd died, mate.
Max   I didn't notice any flowers.
Jeff   You'd not have.
Max   Eh?
Jeff   If you'd died.
Max   So you didn't bother sending any?
Jeff   That's it.
          Swift half down the *Plume,* then, now you're not dead?
Max   Got to ask you something first.
Jeff   Right you are.

Max It's something I promised someone I'd ask.
Jeff What's that then?
Max About *us*.
Jeff What us?
Max You and me, us.
Jeff Eh?

Pause

Max You know when I told you Katie'd left me?
Jeff Right.
Max What did you think?
Jeff What did I think?
Max What did you think?
Jeff I don't think much, mate.
Max You weren't surprised she'd left me?
Jeff No.
Max Why not?
Jeff Cos Kate's all right to look at in all those plays of hers we've had to go to.
And you're not all right to look at in anything.
Max What if I was?
Jeff You'd not be you.
Max That's what I said about you.
Jeff Eh?

Pause

Max When I told you about Kate going…?
Jeff I am getting seriously dehydrated, you do know that?
Max Did you think "I'm not surprised she's left because I've always wondered about Max"?
Jeff "Wondered about Max"?
Max Yes. "I've always thought Max might be a bit…"?
Jeff "A bit…"?
Max "You know"?
Jeff "A bit you know"?
Max Exactly.
Jeff No.

Pause

I could do with a drink.

Max In a minute.

Pause

It's not me this.
Jeff It's not you.
Max Well, it is, but it isn't.
Jeff Right.
Max But I promised.
Jeff You promised.
Max Yes.
Jeff Right. So?
Max So when I told you about Kate leaving me?
Jeff Yes.
Max Why didn't you hug me?
Jeff Hug you?
Max What were you afraid of?
Jeff Afraid of?
Max You're afraid of me, aren't you?
Jeff Why should I be?
Max In case if you hug me I might think something.
Jeff Might you?
Max I don't know. But is that why?
Jeff I've lost you, mate.
Let's go for a gargle?
Max Wait—please?
Jeff I'm waiting.
Max Some people would have hugged me.
Jeff Who?
Max Some people.
Jeff You want some people to hug you now?
Max I don't know!
Jeff Hug you, you say?
Max Yes.
Jeff You want me to hug you now?
Max How can I know till you have?
Jeff What if you don't want me to when I have?
Max I'll know.
Jeff But what about me?
Max What about you?
Jeff What if I don't want to hug you?
Max You won't know till you have.
Jeff But I do know.
And I don't.

Pause

     Max.
Max Yes?
Jeff Got a question for you this time, mate?
Max Good. Anything you like.
Jeff Important question?
Max Go on!
Jeff I'll hold you to it?
Max All right. Ask!
Jeff Handles? Or straight glass? For your pint?
Max I told her.
Jeff Who?
Max Someone.
Jeff Right. You told someone.
     Told them what?

Max shakes his head

     I could murder a pint, if this lot's done with?
Max "One kisses and one turns the cheek."
Jeff You've been at the sauce already.
Max No.
Jeff *Plume of Feathers* next station stop, then.

Daniel enters

     And anyway I'd *heard* about you and Katie. (*He sees Daniel*)
     Hey up, grand-dad.
     Listen, I could probably get you a test drive in that Proton if you're still
     interested? They're clever the Malaysians, well, they've had to be with
     all that jungle.
     Ideal car for senior cits who do a bit of shopping and pubbing?
     Talking of which, we're just nipping down to the *Plume*.
Daniel I'll just nip with you.
Max You'll go home to your wife.
Daniel You've not gone home to *your* wife.
Jeff He's got a point there, mate.
Max He has not got a point there, mate.
     I *am* home.
Jeff My wife left me two years ago.
Max I didn't know that.
Jeff I didn't tell you.

He was a copper.

Max Why?

Jeff It was his job.

Max Why did she leave you?

Jeff No idea.

Max You must have wondered?

Jeff Not much.

She was always a *noisy* woman, I know that.

And I know if I ever meet another one she'll have to listen to me a bit more.

Max Do you *want* to meet another one?

Jeff I'm not sure. What about you?

Max I'm not sure either.

Daniel Me neither.

Jeff (*to Daniel*) You've still got one.

Daniel Aye, but for how long?

Jeff True, you never know.

Give her a spin in that Proton, that'll take her mind off things.

Daniel You understand women, you.

Max and Jeff look at each other

Jeff Beer?

Max Right.

(*To Daniel*) And you keep your hands off my Christmas Drambuie.

Daniel What Christmas Drambuie?

(*He looks, fatally, in the direction of the Drambuie*) I hate Drambuie.

The Lights flicker

Max (*to the audience*) Three weeks *earlier*.

On a Saturday afternoon in late February.

I'm on my third private therapy session with Noon.

Max Johnson's three rules of therapy.

One: it gets dangerous when you stop making jokes.

Two: therapy is like history.

In both you struggle to half remember things everyone else has long forgotten, and you hope no-one'll notice when you start making it up. And...

Three: never say you're sorry.

SCENE 6

Three weeks earlier. A Saturday afternoon in late February

Max and Noon are on stage

Max Sorry.
Noon Why?
Max I was thinking about something else.
Noon You are sorry you were thinking about something else?
Max Yes.
Noon Do you feel you can say what the something else was that you were thinking about?
Max Yes.
     Therapy is like history.
Noon Are you comfortable with that?
Max Yes.
Noon Right.

Pause

     Can you share what you're feeling now, Max?
Max Yes.
     I'm feeling like the Archduke Franz Ferdinand in Sarajevo on June the twenty-eighth, nineteen fourteen.
Noon Can you say why?
Max He got shot.
     And started the First World War.
     He was only the occasion though. Not the cause.
     But *he* didn't really matter at all.

Pause

     I want to be my own cause.
     Not someone else's occasion.
Noon We carry so much baggage.

Pause

Max I want to matter in my own life.
Noon Would you run that past me again?
Max I want to matter in my own life.
Noon Hold on to your wants.

Max Right. I sometimes want to be the cause, not the occasion.
Noon Yes.
      Don't feel other people's feelings, Max.
Max I won't.
Noon Don't be afraid.
Max No.
Noon Love yourself.
Max Thank you.

Long pause. She's not going to speak

      I'm enjoying this.
Noon You're enjoying it?
Max More than I enjoyed those save-our-marriage therapy sessions with you
      Kate made me come to.
Noon You didn't enjoy those?
Max Not really. Sorry.
Noon Don't be sorry.
Max Can I be sorry for being sorry?
Noon Max!

Pause

      Didn't you enjoy those sessions?
Max I didn't mind the arguments we had after, when you'd given us
      something new to argue about.
Noon You enjoyed arguing when you had something new to argue about?
Max Yes.

Pause

      Like the record collection.
      That could have been a brilliant argument.
      We'd never shared it out before, you see.
Noon What did you feel about that?
Max That we used to like some funny music.
      But it was never me who was the Cliff Richard fan.
Noon It wasn't?
Max No, it was not!

Pause

Noon Do you feel you can say what you feel about Cliff Richard?

Max Do you want me to?
Noon If you feel it's what you want?
Max I don't want.
Noon We sometimes have to want, Max.
        If we don't want we don't get, do we?

Pause

Max I wanted someone to take my side.
Noon I think there may be something getting in the way of your feelings.
Max Do you?
Noon Don't you?

Pause

Max My kids wouldn't take sides at all.
Noon You wanted your kids to take sides?
Max I needed someone to.
Noon Haven't you got a best friend?
Max I don't think I have … Jeff maybe?
Noon Jeff?
Max He sells cars and drinks beer.
Noon Jeff's important to you?
Max He's a mate.
Noon A mate?
Max Yes.
Noon In trouble, it's Jeff you turn to?
Max No.
Noon You want to turn to Jeff?
        But you daren't turn to him in case he can't give you what you need?
Max No.
Noon In case he can?
Max No… I don't…

> *During the following, Frank comes on humbly, unseen, finding what he
> thinks is an embarrassing moment*

Noon I feel there are feelings here that can be released, Max. And perhaps
        you can be released from those feelings?

Pause

        In love, Max, there is always one who kisses and one who turns the
        cheek.

Max sees Frank

Frank The door was open, Mr Johnson, only I know Anna isn't in?
Max So?
Frank I just wanted to give you your key back, Mr Johnson.
Max My key?
Frank Yes, sir.

Max takes it

     I haven't used it.
     Anna kept telling me Thursdays is your quiz night at the *Plume*.
     But there's no way I would take advantage, Mr Johnson.
     I don't believe in…
     Not beyond…
     Without commitment.
     And even then all the relevant people would have to approve.
     Sex isn't…
     Thank you and I'm sorry if…
     Good.

   Frank leaves

Max Friend of Anna's.
Noon Returning your key?
Max Yes.

Pause

She waits for Max, but he's not playing

Noon Well.
     OK.
     Do you feel you can say why you feel so strongly about Cliff Richard?
Max Do I?
Noon Don't you feel you do?

Pause

     Let's go back to Jeff, then.
Max Jeff?
Noon Your mate.
Max My mate.

Noon Do you feel we're blocking on Jeff?
Max Are we?
Noon Do you feel we are?

Long pause

      How do you feel about being gay?
Max How would I feel?
Noon How do you feel?
Max If I was gay?
      Do you think I am?
      Wouldn't I know if I am?
Noon Would you?
Max Wouldn't I?
Noon They're your feelings, Max. Own them.

Pause

Max You think I should try out being gay?
Noon What do you think?
Max I think I might not like it when I do?
Noon But at least you'll know.
Max What about the person I've tried it out with?
Noon Jeff?
Max Jeff?
      I'm not gay.

Pause

Noon You might be fighting off the exact deep movement you most need.
Max Might I?
Noon Mightn't you?
Max I might.

Pause

Noon So. What do we know about Jeff?
Max He's married.
Noon Are you comfortable with that?
Max More comfortable than he is probably.
Noon Share some more about Jeff, Max?
Max He's hideous to look at, and I wouldn't dream of buying a car from him.
Noon What would you feel about him if he wasn't hideous to look at?

Max I'd feel it wasn't him I was looking at.
　　　But I'd still not buy a car from him.

Pause

Noon is terribly distressed

Noon You're joking, Max.
　　　Don't joke, Max!
　　　Please don't get stuck.
　　　Some lives get stuck for ever.
　　　Some people crack, Max!
Max Do they?
Noon (*forcefully*) Promise me you'll ask Jeff.
　　　Ask him about *his* feelings?
　　　Tell him yours.
　　　Don't be afraid.
　　　Hug him. Promise you will. Yes?
　　　Next time you see Jeff. Promise!
　　　Hug! Talk!
　　　Promise?
Max Yes, all right, Noon, but——
Noon Cross your heart and hope to die, promise promise?
Max Yes.
Noon Say it.
Max I promise.
Noon Thank you, Max.
　　　Thank you very much.

Pause

　　　You want to matter in your own life?
Max Yes.
Noon It's exactly how *I* feel.
Max You feel that you want to matter in your own life?
Noon Yes.
Max You want to be the occasion not the cause?
Noon Yes.

Pause

Max Is it your—partner?

Noon nods. Max nods

Noon Love shouldn't run out.
        But it always does.
Max (*nodding*) One kisses, one turns the cheek.

Noon nods

Pause

Noon I think there is some movement.
Max Good.
Noon Some deep movement.
Max How can you tell?
Noon We've stopped making jokes, haven't we? (*She crumples*)
        Sorry. Sorry.
Max Don't be sorry for being sorry.
Noon Sorry only…
Max Why shouldn't therapists be unhappy?
        Even historians occasionally get the past wrong.
Noon It's all my baggage, Max.
Max Would hugs help?
Noon Ask Jeff for a hug.
Max I'd rather ask you for a hug.

Pause

Noon How do you feel about asking me for a hug?
Max I feel … comfortable with it.

Pause

Noon Would Katie mind?
Max Why are you asking me about someone else's feelings?

They hug tentatively

        Are you comfortable?
Noon Yes. Are you?
Max Yes.

They hug harder

        (*To the audience*) And the rest … is *history*!

They go towards the bedroom

The Lights flicker

Max Johnson's penultimate rule of history—men are better than women at looking back.
Turn back that clock!
To a Sunday morning a fortnight earlier in mid February.
Emma is in her room. But at any moment she may come out to *stare*.
Anna is tormenting me in person.
And it's not surprising if I am drinking too much.

SCENE 7

A fortnight earlier. A Sunday morning in mid February

Max is drinking beer

Anna is marking the Observer *Soulmates*

Emma is heard making music off

Anna You're drinking too much.
Max It's not surprising.

She smacks the Observer

Anna "Outgoing brunette, twenty-four, into people, music, arts and laughing, hopes to meet a gregarious gorgeous guy for fun times".
Max (*shaking his head*) I'm not gregarious.
Anna Or gorgeous.
"Slim redhead, F forty-two, great sense of humour left wing atheist".
Max God, no.
Anna "Two lonely sculptresses seek man who will be putty in their hands. Sheffield".
Max Sheffield?
Anna "Semi-retired, F fifty, teacher into arts, cinema and home life"?
Max Tried home life.

Pause

Anna That's it then.
So our top three are...
"Wendy still waiting for Peter."

The "Veggie F Arsenal Indie/rock and comedy fan, forty-nine, seeks tall and tactile man who doubts I exist".
And the "Bright feisty fit, F forty-one, f/ship TLC and more in Norfolk"…

A timid knock is heard on the front door

He's come!
Max I'm not lending you any money.
Anna He's not bad in a Cliff Richard sort of way.
Max So don't ask.
Anna I didn't think he'd actually dare come round.
(*She realizes*) And I don't know his name.

Emma plays off

(*She makes to go*) I've got to clean my teeth.
Let him in and talk to him nicely.
Max What about?
Anna Cliff Richard.
Max Cliff Richard?
Anna Mum says he was your favourite.
Max I never even liked Cliff Richard. And your mother——
Anna And find out his *name* for me.

Anna rushes off to get ready

A timid knock again

Max goes out to the front door

Max (*off*) Hallo there.
Do come through, er…
Anna just brushing her teeth in case she has to bite anyone.
Frank (*off*) Mr *Johnson*!
Max (*off*) Yes, that's right.

Max and Frank come in. Frank has a huge bunch of flowers

Frank I knew she was *Anna* Johnson, of course.
She told me.
But I didn't know you were *Mr* Johnson.
Max There's a fair chance? If I'm her father?

And you're...?
Frank Only a friend.
There's nothing going on, Mr Johnson.
Max Quite so.
Those flowers are a lovely old-fashioned idea.
Frank Thank you.
Max Do they have a lovely old-fashioned card to go with them?
To show who they are from?
Frank They're from me, Mr Johnson.
And if it is old-fashioned then call me old-fashioned, but I think young
people today have got it wrong.
Commitment!
Max Quite.
Frank None of this jump into bed business for me.
I don't actually believe in sex beyond marriage.
Do you?
Max It doesn't really arise much for me, beyond or...
Look, I'm terrible with names.
Frank People hardly ever remember mine.
Max Is that because it's difficult?
Frank Do you think it's difficult?
Max No, of course not. But do you think people don't remember it because
it's too easy?
Frank Do you think it is, Mr Johnson?

Pause

Max I think we should have drink.
So.
It's cider you drink these days, isn't it?
Frank I don't drink at all, Mr Johnson, I'm glad to say. Well, I do drink at
all, of course, or I'd be dead.
But I don't drink alcohol.
Max Oh, I do.
Watch! (*He gets a drink*)
Frank The First World War!
Max (*absently*) Mmm?
Frank That was quite interesting.
It took ages.
Max Four years.
Frank I don't think it could have.
Max I am a historian, you know.
Frank Yes, I know you are, of course.

Max So you take my word for it.

First World War, four years.

Five, if you count both ends.

Frank I'm sure it wasn't five.

Max They thought it was going to be over by Christmas.

It might never have happened at all, of course.

Suppose the Archduke hadn't been shot?

Which he wouldn't have been if the roads hadn't been being mended in Sarajevo that summer.

There would have been a war some time but not that one.

History is more than coincidence, of course, or what would be the use of the historian.

But there are certainly coincidences.

Frank Us!

We're coincidences, aren't we?

Max In a sense we——

Frank Or if I'd not been out there checking my mother's Nissan Micra boot just after Christmas?

And this beautiful girl hadn't come rushing out into the road, telling me to take a key and a Cliff Richard record round to her mother's new flat?

Where would *I* be?

Max Not here.

But you'd still be you?

Frank Yes.

Max Your name would still be…?

Frank But I'd not have met Anna's amazing mother?

Max Ah.

Frank She wants me to join her amateur dramatics society!

Max I wouldn't.

Frank She said Anna will be impressed?

Max She won't.

Emma plays a fragment and stops

My daughter.

Frank It's lovely.

Max You like modern music?

Frank If it's not too modern, of course.

Max You like Cliff Richard, though?

Frank Yes, actually.

Very much.

Pause

      I'll go if she's practising.

Max I don't blame you.

Frank But you'll tell her I called.

Max I will.

      I thought it was Anna you'd come for?

Frank It was.

Max Well, that's Emma.

Frank Oh, I thought——

Max Me Max, Emma Emma, Anna Anna, you...?

Frank Me.

      Isn't Anna home?

Max She's just cleaning her teeth for you.

      So we'll just have to keep trying to talk, shan't we?

      So.

      Do you have a job at all?

Frank Boots.

Max Boots?

Frank I work at Boots.

Max Boots!

      I thought you meant boots.

      I've been to Boots, of course.

      (*He realizes*) I bet you have one of those little pin-on cards they have on their lapels at Boots to remind you who you are?

Frank Oh, yes.

Max So, what does yours say?

Frank Who I am, Mr Johnson.

      Please don't *look* at me, Mr Johnson.

      Honestly, there is no way I will ever take advantage of Anna.

Max I wouldn't tell her that.

Anna comes in

      Ah, Anna. Anna, this is——

Frank Anna! Your father's Mr *Johnson*.

Anna I sort of knew that.

Frank You didn't say.

Max I've found out a few things about our young friend, Anna.

      He doesn't drink.

      He doesn't believe in sex.

      Going to be a thin do, Anna.

Frank These are for you.

Anna No-one's ever bought me flowers.

      Look. This is bit awkward.

But I've forgotten your n——

Frank It wasn't awkward. It was wonderful.

As soon as Mr Johnson opened the door I knew he *was* Mr Johnson.
And he said straightaway "Come in, Frank, Anna's cleaning her teeth
in case she has to bite someone".
I knew it was a joke. He was always full of jokes.
"Come in, Frank".

Anna "Come in, Frank"?

Frank Yes. After all this time!
Sir remembered!

Max I taught him!

Anna Frank.

Frank You see, he remembers everything.

Max I'm a historian, you see.

Frank Yes, and we've been talking about the First World War, haven't we,
sir?
Like old times.
Like history.
Now *I've* made a joke!

Anna If he taught you, you'll remember the death of Rasputin then?

Frank No.

Max Why not?

Frank He was when I had my adenoids operation, Mr Johnson. My friend
said he was quite interesting.

Max *Quite?*
He's the best thing since Henry the Eighth.
Sit down, Frank.

Anna Stand up, Frank.

Max It was a cold night in St Petersburg and——

Anna Dad, will you just shut up and lend me——

Frank I just don't think we should talk to our fathers like that, Anna.

Anna Don't you?

Frank No.
I'm sorry but you don't mind me saying what I think, do you, Mr
Johnson?

Max I admire your frank-ness.
Especially about old-fashioned values.
Like no you-know-what beyond marriage.

Frank Thank you, Mr Johnson.

Max And call *me* old-fashioned.
But I expect you prefer to pay when you take a girl out, don't you?

Frank I do.

Max I admire that too.

So a historic moment.
For the first time ever, Anna can go out without asking me for money?
Frank Not that I do take girls out.
Max But now you are doing?
Frank (*formally*) Yes.
I'd like your permission to take Anna out now, sir?

Pause

Max I don't see how she can come to any harm.
Take her away!

Anna gives the flowers to Max

Anna Stick these somewhere.
Frank Thank you so much, Mr Johnson.
Anna (*going off*) I'll be late.
Max I don't think you will, will she, Frank?

Anna starts to drag Frank away

Frank Certainly not, Mr Johnson.

   Anna and Frank exit

The Lights flicker

   Kate comes on and begins to shuffle the record collection

Max just watches

Max The clock goes backwards for the last time.
Six weeks *earlier.*
To the late afternoon, at the end of last Christmas.
Where the story really begins, of course...

SCENE 8

Six weeks earlier. Late afternoon right at the end of last Christmas

Kate is on her knees, sorting out old LP records into piles

Kate *Help*?
You.
10cc?
Me.
Paul Simon?
Me.
Joni Mitchell?
Me.
Van Morrison?
You.
Bowie?
Me.
Bowie?
Me.
Bowie?
Me.
Joe Cocker?
You.
The Carpenters?
Age Concern…
Elkie Brooks?
Me.
Ah look, side by side from when we first put our record collections
together.
Bob Dylan!
You.
Bob Dylan!
Me.
Genesis?
Me.
Kate Bush?
Me.
Death in Venice?
Age Concern.
Jethro Tull?
You.
Cliff Richard?
Definitely you.
Bob Marl——

Max No.

Kate No what?

Max No Cliff Richard.

Kate It's yours.

Max No, Kate.
Kate It was.
Max Not.
Kate You loved Cliff.
Max I hated Cliff.
Kate (*reading*) "M Johnson".
Max Different M Johnson.
Kate "Please return to M Johnson".
Max It's been planted.
Kate It's your writing.
Max Forged.
Kate By whom?
Max You.
Kate Why?
Max You forged everything.
Kate Not "Please steal and melt for an ashtray and never under any circumstances whatever return to M Johnson".
Max You're the one who wanted to actually *see* Cliff.
Kate When?
Max When you were going to London with that friend of yours with the funny leg, but you had shingles, only it wasn't, it was strawberries.

Anna and Emma come on, hand in hand, and watch from a distance

Kate It wasn't the same summer.
Max Maybe not but *it was the same Cliff*!
Kate The one you liked.
Max Never liked him.
Kate Always jealous of him cos he always looks younger than you.
Max Celibacy. I should have tried it.
Kate You couldn't have with me.
         And anyway you took me to that film of his with the red bus? The one with Dandy Nichols?
Max It wasn't Dandy Nichols, it was the daughter.
Kate See? (*She notices the girls*)
         I was just taking one last look at your father's Cliff Richard collection. I don't want any of them actually.
Max Nor me.
Kate Off to Age Concern with the lot.
Anna Mother.
         Father.
         We wish to say something…

Pause

Please.
Don't split up.

Kate We have been over and over it, haven't we?

In all our family meetings?

Surely we've had the shouting and tears?

We *agreed.*

Anna You agreed.

And then kept talking till we were too tired to bother.

Kate In nine months you will be doing Physics at Cambridge.

Emma will be in Upper School.

Dad will surely have got his early retirement by then, or it won't *be* early.

And I shall be coming to the end of my access course for the theatre studies degree, and be ready for the second act of my life.

Wasn't this Christmas horrible enough?

You don't want me and Dad to end up like Grans and Gramps?

Anna It's not just *Dad* you're leaving.

Kate You two know that you have each got a room any time you want in my flat.

Oh, come on!

We might all get a bit of *peace*, this way.

Max, will you just for once try to help?

Max Peace? (*He takes his time*)

The Peace Treaty of Versailles that settled the First World War——

Anna History, Dad?

Max —also started the Second.

Anna While your family blows up?

Max History is a great comfort. It—a—makes some sense and—b— reminds you that other peop——

Anna You two've squabbled for years! Why split up now?

Max When you ask "why?" in history you have to be very careful to distinguish the *occasion* from the *cause.*

Anna Oh, thank you.

That's the history.

So what about you, Mother? I bet you've got a nice relevant bit of a play for us?

Kate Have I?

Oh, yes. Let's see if I can still…

Yes.

Yes. I think I might have. (*She takes her time, then deliberately throws the key*)

"Torvald, I don't believe any longer in wonderful things happening. Goodbye."

      He cries.
      But the last thing you hear is that door slamming.
      For *ever*.
      Henrik Ibsen's *A Doll's House.*
Max Karl Marx says somewhere that history repeats itself.
Anna Plays and history, you two!
Kate We did it six years ago with poor Melissa Trumping.
Anna But you don't feel anything about anything *real*!
Kate I *am* crying, dear.
Anna You're pretending to cry.
Max First it's tragedy…
Kate I really cried the one night I went on for Melissa Trumping.
      She was so pregnant they'd had to remove the door so they couldn't
      have a slam at all.
Max …then it's *farce.*

Pause

Anna Right.
      From now on, you two've had it from us.
Emma I'm never talking to them ever again.

Kate tries to embrace Emma, then Anna

Kate I…

Nobody moves

  Kate exits

They wait for the door to slam. It does

Anna She always comes back because she's always forgotten something.
      Only this time she's forgotten *us*.

Emma picks up Kate's key and gives it to Anna

      Her key. (*She goes to the window*)
      She'd better have it back for when she changes her mind.
Max I don't think this time…
Anna There's that boy with the red car again. (*She waves*)
      He waved back.
      I'll give him her key to here to take round her new flat.

Then she'll shout at him and he'll have to bring it back to me.
Then I'll shout at him and he'll have to take me for a drink and a snog
in his red car.

Max Get him to take this to her as well while you're at it.

Anna What?

Max Her Cliff Richard.

Anna You deserve each other, you two.

Anna hurries out with the record and key

Emma goes to her room

Max turns to her but she's gone

The Lights flicker

Max (*to the audience*) A forgotten key?
Cliff Richard?
A boy in a red car?
A snog?
Max Johnson's last rule of history!
The further back you go … the less it's your fault!
So look back in hope!
Anyone for Rasputin?
We are in Moscow, in the deepest of winters and…

Black-out as Cliff Richard suddenly sings Bachelor Boy

ACT II

Kate's sitting-room. Late last December

The room is in darkness

We hear Kate fumbling at her door, not finding it easy to get in

Kate (*off*) Here we are!

We hear her struggling

> Home at last!

Kate comes into her dark sitting-room

> Stand by elex!
> Three two one and—
> Lights! (*She switches the light on*)

We see that she is unchanged from Act I, except for a bottle of sherry she's bought on her way over. She begins to drink it

The doorbell rings

> I wanna be alone!
> So go away whoever you are or I will be obliged to sell you two tickets for my next appearance on the boards.
> Which is as Nancy Holmes in J B Priestley's *When We Are*——

The doorbell rings again

> Two tickets it will be, then. (*She gets the tickets and goes to answer the door*)
> Your cue to speak, dear?

Frank (*off*) I've been sent round with this Cliff Richard record and——

Kate Speak up or no-one will ever hear you.
Frank (*off*) I have adenoids——

Kate opens the door

——Thank you very much, Mrs Johnson.
Kate I'm not Mrs Johnson.
Frank This was your address.
Kate This is my address.
Rather a bijou flat?
I have just left everything and started the second act of my life alone
here.
Frank Anna said you lived here.
Kate Oh, *Anna*!
Frank So you know Anna?
Kate Can you show me one mother who knows her own daughter?
Frank No, but I am correct in assuming you are Anna Johnson's mother?
Kate You are.
Frank In which case——
Kate You must come in because——
Frank I've only got this key and this rec——
Kate —I've got something for you.
Enter.

He has to

You are my very first visitor, so if I can find any glasses you will have
a small sherry.
Frank I'm afraid I don't drink alcohol.
Kate I'm afraid we always drink small sherries in the amateur theatre.
On stage anyway.
What's your name again?
Frank It's not *again*.
Kate Sorry?
Frank I never told you before, so it can't be *again*.
Frank.
Kate Who is?
Frank Me.
Kate You're frank?
Frank Yes.
Kate It's a rather boring quality in my experience. You always know where
you are with frank people.
Frank I am Frank.
Kate You said.

Frank It's my name. Frank.

Kate Oh, dear.

Frank It wasn't exactly my choice, Mrs Johnson.

Kate That's all right, Frank, because I'm not Mrs Johnson. And that is exactly my choice.

Frank But if you're Anna's——

Kate I have reverted.

Your stage name could be Francis, you know? We have wonderful names in the amateur theatre.

(*She finds a glass for herself*) Ah!

Frank Cliff Richard!

Kate Mmm?

Frank I think he's got that something.

Kate Who?

Frank Cliff.

Kate Cliff?

Frank I do like him.

Kate Then you keep him.

Frank Anna said I must make you take him.

Kate It's time Anna picked on someone her own size.

Frank Anna and I have never spoken before tonight.

I was just out checking if I'd locked my mother's Nissan Micra. I had seen her, of course.

Kate Your mother?

Frank Anna.

Kate Fancy her?

Frank Anna?

Kate Yes.

Frank No.

Kate No?

Frank I'm not that kind of person.

Kate In the theatre, Frank, we can *change* the kind of person we are.

We can actually *become other people*.

Frank I'm sure you can.

Well, I think perhaps I should leave now that I have accomplished my unexpected——

Kate Clumsy people like you can become graceful.

The unlovable become desirable!

Frank Do they?

Kate I'll give you a free sample?

But I'll need that. (*She takes the key*)

"I have put the keys here."

"Nora, shall you never think of me again..."

"I know I shall often think of you and the children and this house."
"Nora!"
"Ah, Torvald, the most wonderful thing of all would have to happen!"
"Nora!"
Bang, crash. The door is heard shutting below.
For ever!
Live performance, Frank.
Nothing is ever so exciting. So…
(*She moves in for the kill, with tickets*) Here you are!
Two tickets for J B Priestley's *When We Are Married*.
Bring Anna!
Going to the theatre is a splendid way of getting off with someone.
All that dark and fumbling behind curtains.
The Saturday night performance. We might know our lines by then.
Six pounds?

Frank Oh. (*He fumbles for his money for ages*)

Kate You've got the bones.

Frank Have I?

Kate But have you got the *blood*?
We're always looking out for new blood.
Tuesday evenings?
(*To the audience*) And a very long twenty-three minutes later, Frank
pays up and leaves *with his two tickets*!
(*To Frank*) I hope that's not somebody out there trying to get into your
mother's Nissan?

Frank Where?

Kate It's a terrible neighbourhood, Frank. They're letting just anyone in
these days.

Frank Where?

Kate There!

Frank Oh!

Kate Yes!

Frank Do you mind if I?

Kate No, you must.

Frank I will. (*He does*) Thanks—Anna's mum.

Kate And thanks for the six pounds.
Frank.

Frank goes

Exit pursued by a bear! (*She drinks to his departure*)

The Lights flicker

She holds up the Cliff Richard record

> "Thou met'st with things dying. I with things new born".
> Shakespeare's *Winter's Tale*.
> (*She hides the Cliff record as she talks*) The very middle of the play just
> after the bear, when everything changes.
> We did a disastrous version with Angelina Darwin as Hermione, and
> we all know why she got the part ... frankly.
> But on with the show.
> We have to look forward in the theatre.
> Always getting nearer to the next opening, of course.
> Undrenchingly optimistic that we'll get it right *next* time.
> Certain that nobody'll notice when we don't.
> And so four weeks nearer,
> On a Tuesday evening in mid February.

SCENE 2

Six weeks later. An evening in mid February

Kate A funny February though.
> First J B Priestley gets postponed until June thanks to Billy Readman's
> court case.
> Then I'm recast as Clara Soppitt, who I'd have thought I'm too young
> for.
> And of course I still wanted to be alone...
> ...When I wanted to be
> But——

The phone rings. The doorbell rings

Emma comes from her room to stare

*Kate wonders if she wants to answer the phone or the door. Neither. She lifts
the receiver and drops it back on the cradle*

Emma goes back to her room

Kate goes to let Anna in

> (*Off*) And why don't you use the key I gave you?
Anna (*off*) I gave it to Frank.

Kate Why would Frank want my key?
Anna That's what he said.
        But I've been staying round Dad's lately anyway.
Kate I noticed.
Anna Did you?

They come in, still talking

Kate Well, sort of noticed. Some of us do have our own lives too, Anna.
Anna Dad's——
Kate Not my problem any more.
Anna (*bringing out the Soulmates page from the* Observer) The *Observer*.
Kate Don't read reviews, dear.
Anna It's the Soulmates page.
        He made me put rings round all the women he's interested in.
Kate He put a ring round this woman when he was interested in her.
        But she turned out to be an escapologist.
        And I'm afraid I have got a rehearsal.
Anna I'm afraid you've got the real thing. (*She reads*)
Kate How *many* women?
Anna You've got a rehearsal.
Kate How *many*?
Anna You're not his problem any more.
Kate I didn't say it that way round.
Anna I did.
Kate How *many*?
Anna He put rings round seven.
Kate Seven?
Anna With question marks over three others.
Kate Ten women in a week doesn't sound quite like your father.
Anna Go round and see him?
Kate Did he send you round to ask me to go round and see him?
Anna No.
Kate But he does want me to go round and see him?
Anna No.

Pause

Kate I think it's all rather naff. Touting yourself round the small ads as if
        you're an old fridge in the post office window.
        What kind of women was he interested in?

Anna takes her time

Anna "Wendy still waiting for Peter. Thirty-seven to forty. Rooftops of
London to explore art, coffee and cake."
Kate Coffee and cake?
Rather than his usual lagoons of alcohol? Next!
Anna "Thirty-seven attractive blond and petite"——
Kate Thirty-seven again?
Anna —"seeks attractive M thirty to thirty-eight in similar"——
Kate He's *not* thirty to thirty-eight.
He thinks just because he didn't grow up he didn't grow old.
Next!
Anna "Veggie F Arsenal Indie/rock and comedy fan, forty-nine, seeks
equally stimulating slim tall and tactile man who doubts I exist."
Kate Me too. Next.
Anna Two rings. "Bright feisty fit, F forty-one, works in the arts. Passionate
about theatre and travel. WLTM M with GSOH for f/ship TLC and
more. Norfolk."
Kate GSOH?
Anna Good sense of humour.
Kate Who has got to have it, her or him?
Anna Him.
Kate That's all right. All men think they're funny.
Anna And I looked up "feisty" and it means——
Kate I know exactly what feisty means, dear.
I *am* feisty.
And since when did your father actually want a feisty woman passionate
about theatre and travel? I've been one for twenty years. He could have
had TLC and more *at home*.
Anna Perhaps he prefers Norfolk?
Kate Very flat Norfolk.
Anna What?
Kate It's from a play.
Anna Everything you say is.

Emma starts her music, off

Emma still tormenting you, then?
Kate Doesn't she play at home?
Anna We haven't got a home.
Kate At Max's?
Anna Oh, she plays all the time there.
Kate Does she speak to him?
Anna Course not.
I think I'll have a shower.

Kate Feel free.
Anna I thought that was the idea.
          I really came for the phone number of that therapist friend of yours with
          the funny name?
Kate Noon? Why?
Anna I know somebody who's unhappy.

Anna goes

Kate "Oh, it's me that hasn't to be silly, is it?
          I suppose standing there with my 'usband's arm round you bold as
          brass, that isn't being silly, is it? I wonder what you call that sort of
          behaviour then?"
          (*She consults her script and shouts the lines against Emma's music*)
          "Oh—an' how long have you been 'aving these bits o' fun—as you call
          them—Herbert Soppitt?"

The Lights flicker

          And on we go
          Ever hopeful that we'll know what to do next, if we get the right cues.
          A few days later.
          On a Saturday morning in February
          A *young man* drops in uninvited.

SCENE 3

A few days later. A Saturday morning in February

Kate reads her When We Are Married

Frank enters

Frank I'm really sorry but the door was open.
Kate It's all right, it's only you.
Frank Anna isn't here, is she?
Kate Don't think so.
Frank Good.

Pause

*Kate goes on doing her words. But when she looks up, Frank speaks with
concern*

You know Anna?

Kate Not much.

We human beings are so terribly separate, aren't we?

That's why I love the theatre.

Frank And I love A——

Kate For two hours we can sit in the dark pretending we're all in the same play all hoping for the same happy ending.

Frank I think you put that very well. But I——

Kate But really, of course, we're all in several different plays, all at the same time.

And most of us only ever get the smallest parts in any of them.

Even our own.

Frank I love An——!

Kate For example, whenever are *you* centre stage?

Frank I love Anna!

Kate Exactly. But you're hardly ever even on stage with her.

Frank I love her!

Kate You're telling the wrong person in the wrong play.

And you've got some rotten lines.

Frank Please listen, Anna's mum?

Kate Yes.

I will.

There's a certain quality of listening on stage that is the mark of the real actor.

Pause

Frank I did tell her I love her.

Kate And?

Frank She was terribly cross.

Kate You've come round this morning to make her terribly cross again.

Frank No.

I came round to bring you this. (*He produces a key*)

Kate Another key?

My key?

Frank Anna's key?

I told her. I told Mr Johnson. I told you.

There is no way I...

It would have been simply *wrong* to come round here to your flat to be alone with her every Tuesday evening when you're at rehearsal.

She doesn't *love* me.

Kate So *you* can't...?

Frank I won't!

Kate No love, no…?
Frank I simply won't.
Kate And Anna is terribly cross about that too?
Frank Terribly.
    She says we should just *carry on*.
    But I will not take advantage of her.
Kate Even if she wants you to?
Frank Exactly.
Kate But if she did love you?
Frank Even then we would have needed to talk it through properly.
    With all the relevant people.

Kate takes the key

Kate If she ever does tell you she loves you?
Frank Yes?
Kate And the relevant people agree?
Frank Yes?
Kate Or if ever you want to hear my Nora and Torvald again?
Frank Thank you. But——
Kate I know where the key is. (*She cuddles him*)
Frank Thanks. For being so understanding.
Kate I don't understand anything. Except in plays.
    (*She holds him theatrically*) And now we are saying goodbye, aren't
    we?
Frank Yes, Anna's mum!
Kate Oh! (*She holds the moment then changes everything*)
    You go round to Mr Johnson's house, of course?
Frank Only when Mr Johnson is in!
Kate Goes without saying, Frank.
    Is he happy?
Frank He's always making jokes.
Kate Not the same thing.
    Does he have lots of girls staying?
Frank Anna stays with him sometimes. And Emma?
Kate I mean *women* girls.
    Try to be frank, Frank.
    Staying-for-breakfast women girls? Who look as if they might read the
    Observer newspaper?
    Who leave dental floss and tights all over my bathroom?
Frank I try not to use other people's bathrooms, Anna's mum.
    But I'd like to leave now in case Anna returns.
Kate Good timing.

Frank makes to go

     I'll get you your rescheduled tickets for the play via Anna.
Frank (*off*) I'm not sure I'll be seeing Anna.
Kate I'm sure you will.
     History repeats itself.
     First tragedy.
     Then farce.
     Max said.
     Or Marx said. Or Max said Marx said.
     Listen to that for articulation.
     Mark this. Marx didn't say Max said Marx said but Max said——

The phone rings

The Lights flicker

     (*To the audience*) And onwards we go, every day a day nearer the
moment the curtains struggle apart and we're on!
     A few weeks later, on a March evening.

SCENE 4

A few weeks later. A March evening

Kate picks up the phone

Emma starts playing, off

Kate Kate Elm.
     Well, I'm Kate Elm now…
     And I don't think you've sorted out your tickets for our rescheduled
J B P yet, have you?
     The first week in June…
     A drink…?

Emma's music stops

     I suppose I'm a bit surprised you rang, that's all…
     Friday'd be lovely. Oh no!

But she is acting

Friday.
Oh, look, it's in the diary!
I've got these two tickets for that new play in *Manchester*. I was going to invite little Emma but she's taking her grades.
Tell you what, why don't you come instead? I've got to do the driving anyway?…
The same little Peugeot…
No, I'm quite happy with the way it starts, thank you…
I've not had any trouble whatsoever, with second gear. But…
Well, you can explain that over supper after?

Emma comes on, staring

I've got to go now. I'm being a teeny bit upstaged. (*She puts the phone down*)
Anyone can stare at people, Emma.
Remember Hermione in Shakespeare's *A Winter's Tale*?
She turns herself into a statue to spite her family and she stays like it for *sixteen years*.
And misses all the second half.
Now I, of course, would have been Hermione, but for Angelina Darwin and we all know why *she* got the part, dear. And what happened to her in the dressing room in the second half.
Every night of the run.

Emma is unimpressed

Talk or go to your room.

Emma turns to go to her room

I've been invited out to the theatre, that's all. There'll come a time in your life when you'll think you'll never get the parts again.

But Emma has gone

Wonderful what a bit of slap can do, though.
On with the motley! (*She gets out her make-up and begins to improve herself*)

Emma plays, then stops

The Lights flicker

And on that Friday in early March, exit Kate E——

Angry Mother's doorbell

SCENE 5

A few days later. That Friday, in early March

Emma's playing resumes

Kate The door is open—Mother.

The doorbell rings again

> My mother would be an awesome Lady Bracknell.
> Certainly rather more so than our own dear Lorraine Painter-Calthrop
> since she got her new teeth.

The doorbell rings again

Emma's music stops

> *Kate goes out*

> *Emma comes in from her room with her instrument, and her teen magazine*

Jenny (*off*) You look a sight.
Kate (*off*) I'm just about to go out to see a play in Manchester.
Jenny You've played your life away.
> (*To Emma*) Still holding your parents hostage?
> Good.
> Parents these days are a disgrace.
> (*To Kate*) And I'm not at the moment referring to what *your* father does
> with my towels.

> *Kate goes out for her coat*

> Who are you going to this play with?
> Only theatre critics and the sexually-wounded go to the theatre on their
> own.
> You're going with a man or you wouldn't be in such a rush.
Kate (*off*) I am in a rush, Mother, yes.

Jenny You're all rush these days. No *stickability*.
Kate (*off*) I am going out.
Jenny Going out never solves anything.
　　　You always have to come back.
Kate (*off*) Not necessarily.
Jenny And I've got two casseroles in the car.
　　　Your father and I haven't had what our doctor calls a full married life
　　　for nine years. You do know that?
Kate (*off*) You've told me often enough. I'm now going——
Jenny Is that what's wrong with Max? Because these days there are CD-
　　　Roms…
　　　And I'm sure even you could try to be a little more pleasant towards
　　　bedtime?

Kate comes back with her coat

Kate Mother, I am now going to Manchester.
Jenny (*to Emma*) Then you had better come with me.
　　　I'll buy some bananas on the way.
　　　We never had bananas but nobody complained.
　　　(*To Kate*) And you can stuff your beef casseroles.
Kate Mother, for the last twenty-three years I have been a vegetar——
Jenny And we'll get some beefburgers on our way to see your sad old father.
　　　If some people are still worried about BSE and eating the world and
　　　global warnings, some people might take a bit more care about the
　　　people they ought to care about first.

Emma whispers to Jenny

　　　And a fillet o' fish.
　　　Quick now before she starts confusing you. She has a nasty habit of
　　　talking.

Jenny and Emma exit fast

The Lights flicker

Kate And at last I go to Manchester!
　　　And at twenty past two in the morning I get *back* from Manchester.
　　　When I do I am surprised to find a light on in my sitting-room.
　　　I do not enter at once…

The Lights flicker

(*She whispers*) A very early Saturday morning
In March.

SCENE 6

Very early on a Saturday morning in March

Anna and Frank are there, in the dim Lighting

Anna I do.
Frank You don't.
Anna Do.
Frank Don't.
Anna Do.
Frank If you did you wouldn't keep asking.
Anna A lot.
Frank Don't.
Anna Do.
Frank It's not respect.
Anna It is respect.
Frank It's not enough.
Anna For you.
Frank For us.
Anna It's more than enough for me.

Pause

Try again.
I fancy you, Frank.
Frank Fancying's not the same.
Anna It usually works.
Frank Not for us.

Pause

Anna My mother goes to some hotel in Manchester for the night with some
feller or other.
So I invite you back at two o'clock in the morning.
So you come.
So?
Frank No.

Pause

Anna——
Anna Here we go again.
Frank I love you.
Anna Not listening.
Frank But unless you love *me* back I'm not even going to contemplate——

We notice Kate is at the door

Anna You do not love me, Frank.
You do not know me, Frank.
I warn you now and for ever, Frank.
Never say anything about *loving* me ever again.
Frank I love you!
Anna Look at our parents and the mess they're all in because they once told
each other *they* loved each other.
When they never even knew each other.
Love's an excuse for getting other people to do things they don't want
to do.
Now take advantage of me or go home. (*She notices Kate*)
Nice timing, Mother.
Kate As always.
Anna I thought you were staying the night in a hotel in Manchester?
Frank I wasn't taking advantage of Anna——
Kate I'm sure you weren't.
Frank How was the play?
Kate The scenery didn't move for me. But——

Jeff blinks into view

This is Jeff. He isn't too keen on theatre.
Jeff People always seem to *say* so much.
Kate Jeff doesn't like saying much. He's a man, Frank.
Anna He's my father's *best friend* actually, Frank.
Jeff There aren't many Franks these days.
Frank It was my parents' idea.
Well, my mother's.
I never had a father.
Well, I must have had a father or I wouldn't be here.
But he wasn't a real father.
Well, he was a real father in the sense that——
Anna Come on, Frank, you're driving me home.
Jeff What are you running at the moment?
Anna His mother's Nissan Micra. Come on.

Jeff The earlier models aren't reliable if they've only had intermittent servicing. And the cam belt can be a bit of a prob——
Anna We've gone, Frank.

Anna exits

Jeff I'd try a little Italian job myself, maybe a Fiat.
Frank I'll tell Mother.
  And I won't take advantage of——
Kate Night, Frank.
Frank Good. Er.
Anna (*off*) Night, Frank.

Frank follows Anna off

Kate Thank you.
Jeff What for?
Kate Tonight?
Jeff I'm sorry, I...
Kate Sorry?
Jeff It is a smooth drive in those little Peugeots.
Kate Do you always get so sleepy or is it just me?
Jeff Oh, it's not you. You don't make any difference.
Kate Oh, good.
  Right. Coffee.
Jeff I daren't at night.
  Keeps me awake.
Kate And you don't like being awake much, do you?
Jeff I only came in because I wanted to say I was sorry.
Kate I never say sorry.
  Except when I forget my lines.
  Need a prompt.
  Don't know what to do next.
  Like now...
  Sorry?
Jeff *Were* you going to stay the night in a hotel in Manchester? Only——
Kate You shouldn't listen in to other people's conversations.
Jeff Why didn't you say?
Kate Why didn't you ask?
Jeff How would I have got back?
Kate You couldn't have.
Jeff Oh.
Kate Yes.

Jeff   But you changed your mind?

Kate   I sort of forgot.

Jeff   Was it my snoring?

Kate   Not at all.

I've given twenty of my best years to the amateur theatre movement.
Snoring men have never stopped me performing yet.

When you rang me up to ask me for a drink?

Jeff   Yes?

Kate   Didn't you think I'd remember you are my estranged husband's best
friend?

Jeff   That's what I wanted to talk about, to be honest.

Kate   What "that"?

Jeff   Max, to be honest.

Kate   You might have said. To be honest.

Jeff   I'm not very good at saying things.

But I used to be married, so I thought it would be all right.

Kate   I'm going to start again.

Weren't you at all surprised when I said I'd got tickets for a show in
Manchester and would you like to come?

Jeff   No.

Kate   No?

Jeff   You've been making us come to plays we don't want to come to for
years, to be——

Kate   —Honest.

Jeff   Yes.

Kate   So you came——

Jeff   Yes.

Kate   —hoping to talk to me about Max?

Jeff   Yes.

Kate   But Max wasn't why I'd invited you to Manchester?

Jeff   No.

Pause

Were you physically attracted to me?

Kate   Not a lot.

Jeff   No, well.

Kate   You to me?

Jeff   A bit.

More like a sister-in-law, to be hon——

Pause

Kate   Tell me about Max?

Jeff It's embarrassing.
Kate Good.

Pause

Jeff I was round his house.
Kate Yes?
Jeff He asked me to *hug* him.
Kate Max did?
Jeff Yes.
Kate My Max?
Jeff Yes.
Kate What did you do?
Jeff Took him for a drink.
Kate Like you do.
Jeff But what he did then?
Kate What?
Jeff He put his hand on my knee.
Kate He very rarely put his hand on my knee.
Jeff In the *Plume*.
Kate Never in the *Plume*.
Jeff I made out I'd not noticed.
Kate Best thing.
Jeff But then he went on and on about my former wife and her policeman.
And asked me if I thought he was gay.
Kate The policeman?
Jeff No, Max.
Kate Max?
Jeff Max asked me if he, Max, was gay?
Kate Sorry?
Jeff Is he?
Gay?
Your husband?
Kate The last I heard, my husband Max was writing letters to disgusting women from a Sunday newspaper.
Do *you* think he's gay?
Jeff I don't think I'd *know*?
If *I'm* not?
Kate And you're not?
Jeff I don't think I am.
Being in the motor trade, for starters.
Kate That's a relief or it would have been yet another completely wasted night at the theatre, wouldn't it?

Jeff I'm sorry about that.

Kate It *is* a shame you don't like theatre, Jeff.
This has a touch of Joe Orton's *Entertaining Mr Sloane* about it. And you're the big boy in the middle of the bed.

Jeff Am I?

Kate Don't worry, our Committee vetoed it.
Too close to home.

Jeff Right we are, then.

Kate So what did *you* say?

Jeff When?

Kate When he asked you if you thought he was gay.

Jeff I bought another round.
Is he?

Kate I don't mind if he is gay.
Why should I mind?
The more people who keep each other warm in a cold world the better.
Gay men are more fun anyway.
I don't mind. It's none of my business.
But I do mind that *he tells you first*!

Pause

Jeff Changing the subject for a minute, and just thinking about your Peugeot?
Do you want me to keep an eye out for a later model?

Kate What I *want*.
To be honest.

Jeff Only the one-oh-six diesel is worth looking at?
The one-point-four is a bit frail.
But you can't really go wrong with the one-point-five?

Kate Is to go wrong with you? (*She steers him to bed*)
Only I think that as long as we're not attracted to each other, it can't really matter if we have a little test drive?

She goes in with him

The Lights flicker

SCENE 7

Several weeks later. A Sunday morning in May

The doorbell rings, then after a pause, it rings again

Jenny (*off*) It's open, of course.
> But you're a very good boy to give me a lift, Frank.
> I sold Gramps' car for scrap, you see.
> Won't need a car now ever again.

Jenny comes into the room

> Anybody home?
> Cos I am.
> Bring them in here.

Frank enters with too much luggage

> (*She unwraps him a toffee*) You've earned your toffee, Frank. (*She pops it in his mouth*)

Frank Thanks.
Jenny And you chew it.

And, chewing, Frank goes out for some more bags

> I'll come out and tell you what to do.
> I've always liked shouting at workmen in the street. Especially men from the council. It's how I met Gramps, of course.

Jenny goes out

Kate comes in

Kate Several weeks closer now.
> A Sunday morning in May.
> Coming up to the crunch.
> Sixteen days to opening night and Lorraine Painter-Calthrop has her usual trouble.
> So we've still never been able to *move* the third act.
> (*She sees her mother's luggage*) No!

Jenny comes in with a wash bag

> No!

Jenny Gin, dear.
> I have been a very brave woman this morning.
Kate Not got any gin.
Jenny (*pointing at a bottle*) That's gin.

Kate That's for the after-show party.

Always supposing there is a show to be after.

Jenny It's part of my revised life plan to join in your amateur dramatics, dear.

Mothers and daughters have to share and bond.

We did it at my widows' group.

So a *large gin* to celebrate.

Kate No!

Jenny You'll need one.

Kate I always do.

Emma's music starts and stops

   Frank comes in with more luggage

Frank Shall I put these…

Kate No.

Frank Hallo, Mrs…

Kate Goodbye, Mister.

Jenny (*to Kate*) He was hanging around outside Max's house.

He agreed to drive me here in return for a toffee.

(*To Frank*) Take my bags through to the little room with the E on the door.

Kate Don't!

A moment of indecision

   But Anna appears

Frank I didn't know you'd be here.

Anna Well, I am.

Frank I'd not have come.

Anna How are you?

Frank Fine. You?

Anna Fine. I suppose.

Jenny If you don't mind, he's in the middle of putting your Grans' bags in my new——

Kate He's actually in the middle of taking your Grans' bags back to your Grans' house.

Jenny Your Grans hasn't got a house.

Frank Are you keeping busy?

Anna Yes. You?

Frank Fairly busy.

And the following two conversations happen more or less at the same time

Jenny Grans is moving in.
Kate Grans is not moving in.
Jenny She already has.
Kate She didn't ask.
Jenny You would have said no.
Kate We've already said goodbye,
Mother.
Jenny If you think you ever say
goodbye to your mother you'll
find you're mistaken.
Kate Twenty-two years ago.
Jenny You get clawed back. Your
family gets older as well, you see.

It'll not be for ever, dear.
One of us will die.
Then we'll see.

Anna How's your mum's Micra?
Frank That man from Manchester
is still very keen for her to trade it
in for a Fiat. He says you know
where you are with the Italians
with them having the Pope.
Anna I hope she doesn't trade it in.
Frank I hope not as well. Have you
found anyone else yet?
Anna Not yet. Have you?
Frank Not really. Not at all, actually.

Emma appears

Your Grans has come to live here.
But you must *say* if that's not OK?

Emma smiles

Good.
You could share a room with me but I am a widow and I think it would
be more proper for you to share with your mother.
(*She signals Frank to deliver the bags*) On your way, José!

Frank goes in

I've put the house on the market at eight grand less than the estate agent
said it could get.
Gramps will be cross but men do get so agitated about money, once
they run out of testosterone, don't they?
Still, we don't need to have anything to do with men from now on, do
we?

Frank comes back

And the next, José.
Anna Don't hurt yourself.
Frank Why would it matter to you if I did hurt myself?

Anna It would hurt me too.
Frank Why?
Anna Because I…
Frank Because you…
Jenny Because men are useless.
Keep going you, you took that toffee.

Frank goes out again

Sisters together under a bloody moon, brown roll-up fags and never again having to put down your own seat.
Oh, don't look so assertive, Kate. Of course you don't want me coming to live here.
Kate No, and you c——
Jenny *You* started off this game of family musical chairs. But it'll take a real woman to finish it.
First though, I am going to wash a man right out of my hair in your shower. (*She goes towards the door*)
I've left Gramps, Anna.
Anna He left you weeks ago.
Jenny Nobody ever left me.
Kate I did.
Jenny You thought you did. Which is different.

Frank comes back in

Frank Anna?
Anna What, Frank?
Frank I think I've lost a filling with that toffee.
Anna Oh, poor Frank! (*She looks in his mouth*)
Jenny I haven't brought a towel.
They all went to Age Concern.
Borrow yours, Kate? (*She heads for the shower*)
Kate (*to Frank*) Take her stuff straight back to her house while she's in the shower.
Jenny (*off*) The estate agent's got the only key.
Kate Take it!

Frank takes a bag off

Anna nearly follows him

We're in Anton Chekhov's *The Three Sisters* now, of course.

"If I lived in Moscow I don't think I'd care what the weather was like".
But we never do get to Moscow, do we?

Anna You got to Manchester.

Kate Not really.

Jenny (*off*) One very large gin!

Kate No no no no!

Anna You're overacting again.

Kate Hardly surprising. Imagine *me* coming to live with *you*?
For ever?

Anna No thanks.

Kate Would you just tell your mother to go?

Anna Yes.

Kate Would she?

Anna No.
But I'm trying to work something out, Mother.

Kate So what *would* you do with your mother if she came to live with you?
You'd kill her.
Good idea.
How though?
By drowning?
Stabbing?
Shooting?
Take her round to Age Concern and leave her there?
Poison her tea?
Gramps has been trying that for years.
Life membership of the Voluntary Euthanasia Society then?

Emma plays

I know.
I'll ask Max——

Anna He's already got Gramps.

Kate —to *bore* her to death with the longest version of the Death of Rasputin.

Anna You miss him.

Kate I've never been to Moscow, so how could I?

Anna *Max!*

Kate Oh, him.

Anna You haven't even spoken.

Kate You mucked things up with Frank.

Anna It's so sad.

Kate Talking of sad... (*She hands Anna her script*)

Anna *Should* I tell him I love him?

Kate I wouldn't.

Anna Even if I do?
Kate In *plays* once one character tells the other they love them,
        they're never as interesting again.
        But don't ask me about real life.
        Halfway down sixty-five.
        "Oh—it's me that hasn't to be silly, is it?
        I suppose standing there with my 'usband's arm round you bold as
        brass, that isn't being silly, is it? I wonder what you call that sort of
        behaviour then?"
        Sorry?
Anna (*prompting*) "Oh—an' how long…"

The Lights flicker

Kate "Oh—and how long have you been 'aving these bits o' fun—as you
        call them—Herbert Soppitt?"

   Anna leaves

        (*To the audience*) And then. A fortnight nearer.
        The show!
        And then the saddest of all days.
        The Sunday *after* the show.

The Lights flicker

SCENE 8

A fortnight later. A Sunday afternoon in the middle of June

Kate Which went very well, thank you for asking.
        Oh, and thank you to all my friends who bought tickets, but couldn't
        make it at the last minute.
        And sorry about J Jonathan Crosby's Ormonroyd in Act Three who
        thought he had been there before.
        And had.
        And did Torquay twice.
        But nobody noticed.

   Anna and Emma come in and move things for the coming meeting

   Noon comes in and massages Kate

The next task now is the family meeting.
One item on the agenda.
Get rid of Grans.
Sharing the afternoon with us—healer, crystals therapist, and alternative masseur, my friend and teacher—Noon.

Noon Here? Oh, sorry.
Kate You're very good, Noon.
Noon I'm not very good, Kate.
I'm not good at all.
In fact, there's something really bad I must tell you.
Kate Mmmm.
Noon Honesty matters.
We have to share to dare.
Dare to share I mean.
Dare to…

Pause

It's about Max.
Kate I know about Max.
Noon You know?
Kate Course.
Noon He told you?
Kate We haven't spoken for six months.
Noon So how can you know about him and——
Kate Though he did come to see the play last week which is more than some people managed.
Noon I'm sorry about that, Kate.
But with this baggage I'm carrying?
Kate Don't be sorry.
Heal!
Noon About Max.
What I did, Kate——
Kate I was surprised, of course.

Pause

Noon Of course you were.
Kate I was.
Noon So was I.
Kate How could you be?
Noon I didn't want it to happen.
Kate Couldn't do much about it, could you?

Noon No, Kate.

Pause

What do you feel about it now?

Kate Nothing.

Noon You're a very generous person with your feelings, Kate, but something terribly wrong did happen?

Kate Not these days.

I just think Jeff wasn't quite ready yet.

Noon Jeff?

Kate Jeff.

Noon Max's friend Jeff? The hideous Jeff?

Kate He is rather hideous, isn't he.

Didn't seem to stop Max though.

Noon Max?

Kate Max.

Noon Jeff?

Kate I agree. He's a bit of a surprise.

I mean he's in the motor trade for starters.

Pause

Noon What about me?

Kate You?

You're a bit stressed, Noon?

Noon Am I?

Yes, I am.

I definitely am. I am.

But Kate, about me and Max?

I'm so sorry.

Kate No point in being sorry.

Noon No, sorry.

Sorry.

Kate (*to the audience*) Also present at this historic meeting—my two wonderful daughters Anna and Emma.

And Anna lets Jeff in with a can of beer

And Jeff.

Who finds Noon's car more interesting than most people would.

Jeff Yes, well, you see the 2CV's very basic and you do have to watch out for that rust in the chassis terminal.

But that's the French for you. I mean look at Vincent van Gogh to name
but three?

Kate He looks after my Peugeot, Noon.

Noon Does he?

Kate But we aren't attracted to each other, so it doesn't matter.

Jeff I get terrific gyp with *my* shoulder, there.

Kate Get Noon to do you.

Jeff I might.

Kate If you want.

Jeff I do want.

Kate If we don't ask for what we want we can't grumble when we don't get
what we want. Right, Noon?

Noon Oh, yes.

Jeff Well, in terms of motors, er, Noon, er, what you want is to cut your
losses and go for a VW.

Noon Oh.

Jeff Trust the Germans. Sausage, beer, Mozart. Ja wohl.
I'm Jeff, by the way.

Noon Jeff!

Jeff Jeff by name, Jeff by nature.

Noon Max's friend Jeff?

Jeff Right.

Noon You're not hideous.

Jeff Thanks.

Noon But you are Max's friend?

Jeff Friendly type, Noon. Say it myself.

Noon I can see why Max is attracted to you.

Jeff Pardon.
I mean sorry, sorry.

Noon We mustn't be sorry.

And they are in love

No point in being sorry, is there, Kate?

Kate Sorry?

Noon Being sorry.

Kate No. Right.
(*To the audience*) Next on—Grans with salad to stave off hunger till
tea.
Which will be salad.

Jenny enters with salad

Jenny I've lost a stone and a half since I gave up men.

But I'm paying for it in wind.

Kate (*to the audience*) A red Nissan Micra draws up outside.

Jenny Now what do you want me in here for?

Kate (*to the audience*) A young chemist's assistant and an angry old man get out.

Jenny Are we going to play a nice game? And then have early tea?

Kate And the scene is set!

Thanks, Noon.

Noon I feel we can forget about Max, Kate?

Kate I have.

Everyone sitting comfortably?

Then we'll begin.

Daniel comes in with Frank

Frank I'll wait in Mum's Nissan.

Jeff Tell her I've still got that yellow Fiat Bravo one-point-six.

Frank Thanks, I'll——

Anna Stay! If you want?

Frank All right.

Anna Sit next to me. If you want?

Frank Sure.

Daniel Young laddo here said it were some kind of secret party.

Well, I'm always ready for it.

Jenny He never *was*.

Daniel sees Jenny

Daniel *She's* here. (*He turns to go*)

Jenny Actually she is *not* here.

She is leaving. (*She gets up to go*)

Daniel I'll stay then. (*He sits*)

Anna Sit down, Grans.

Jenny Not in the same room as a certain person.

Daniel Nor me, not never again.

Jenny He means not *ever* again, of course. But he thinks double negatives are clever.

Daniel Not never hag-ain.

Jenny He thinks that's clever too, putting his aitches in the wrong place. And calling them haitches.

Daniel Haitch.

Jenny Exactly.

He begins to go, so she sits

Anna Sit down, Gramps. Next to me, like when I was Gramps's little girl?
Jenny If a certain person does sit down——
Daniel Haitch. (*He sits*)

Jenny stands up

Kate Sit down, Mother.

Jenny sits. Daniel makes a token effort to stand

Jenny I hope a certain person——
Daniel This certain person——
Anna Shush, you two.
Jenny Nice.
Daniel Very nice.
Anna Mum?
Kate Right, everyone. Now this is Noon.
Daniel What is?
Noon I am.
Kate She's sharing the afternoon with us.
Jenny Noon?
Noon It's my name.
Jenny It's a silly name.
Jeff I like it. Be a brilliant name for a little one-oh-six.
Jenny How can anyone share an afternoon?
Daniel High Noon!
I bet a lot people say that, don't they?
Noon I don't mind, Gramps.
Daniel I mind Gramps.
Noon You mind Gramps?
Jenny And so say all of us.
Daniel It was a certain person's doing.
The day Kate had her first baby that certain person just started calling me *Gramps*.
She never asked me.
Well, I'm never going to answer to *Gramps* again!
Jenny Gramps!
Daniel Don't you talk to me never again, you——
Jenny See? It knows its own name!
Noon Who are you going to be instead?
Daniel Daniel.
Jenny No-one *ever* called him Daniel.
Noon Hi Daniel?

Daniel Hi. Noon.

Jenny (*scoffing*) Daniel!

Daniel A certain person would never use my proper name. But what she never noticed was I'd stopped calling her any names at all.

Jenny She did notice.

Daniel Just like she never noticed when I pulled faces at her.

Jenny And the wind caught him and he stayed like it.

Daniel Or when I made her tea with bath water.

Jenny Dan Dan the dirty old man who washed his face in a frying pan.

Daniel Didn't!

Jenny There's not a man in England who can leave a towel like him.

Kate Noon?

Would you like to start us...?

Noon Yes.

Good.

Now I wonder if we would all be comfortable if we started by doing the opening circle?

We simply go round and each of us says what we'd like to get out of this session?

So who feels that they can start us off? (*She looks encouragingly round*)

Immediately Jenny and Daniel are off again

Jenny		Old men get old much faster than us. See them in the supermarkets muttering abuse at their wives through their wobbly teeth, all thin little legs and arms and dripping everywhere. And course they know they're going to die first, bound to turn them nasty.
(*together*)	
Daniel		Oh, listen, I thought I heard something. Was it a teacher's fingers scraping down the blackboard? Was it a bird with its beak trapped and ripping in a barbed wire fence? Is it the sound of a nail file rasping at an old man's infected toe nail? Or could it be an old wife scratching herself in a vinegar bath, with a dry loofah.

Noon Shut up!

Both of you!

Shut up! Shut up, shut up, shut up!

They do

I'm sorry.

I shouldn't have.

It's absolutely…
I am so sorry.
I'll go now. (*She is on her way out*)

Jeff gets up

Jeff I'll show you what I think I can do for you with your motor, Noon, if
you're done with this job?

Jeff leaves first

Kate (*to the audience*) There's a wonderful scene at the end of William
Shakespeare's *As You Like It*.
We used to do proper plays once, five or six a year.
And I was Hymen actually.
Anna You were brilliant, Noon.
Noon I'm so *sorry*!
Anna Wasn't she brilliant, everyone?
Noon I should never have——
Kate (*to the audience*) And everything is still all muddled up and it's only
about five minutes before the end and you wonder how it'll possibly
all get sorted.
Noon Was I…?
Do you feel I…?
Maybe I…?
Do we think we *can* work through this?
Through the pain to the gain?
Only sometimes if there is to be movement—any deep movement?
Anna Go for it!

Jeff comes in

Jeff Noon?
Kate And I just step into the middle and move them all around
"Peace, ho, I bar confusion.
'Tis I must make conclusion
Of these most strange events.
Here's eight that must take hands
To join in Hymen's bands,
If truth holds true contents."
Then I pair them all off
Orlando and Rosalind
Oliver and Celia

Phoebe and Silvius
Touchstone and Audrey.
Then I sing.
But I won't.

And she doesn't

Noon (*immediately*) Daniel?
Daniel Mmmm.
Noon Do you think you can share your feelings with us?
Daniel I'm so tired.
Noon Tired?
Daniel I don't sleep, any more.
You get used to people breathing next to you.
Even when you don't want them to.
Noon What do you feel you want, Daniel?
Daniel I want to go home.
Noon You feel … you want to go home.
Daniel I *know* I want to go home.
Noon Hugs! (*She hugs him*)
Daniel Mmmmmm…
Jenny What's he mean mmmmmmm?
Noon How do you feel about asking him?
Jenny And what's he mean by *home*?
Kate (*to the audience*) And Noon does her big speech.
Noon We all want to go home.
We all grieve for our lost selves.
For ever.
We are all orphaned from our own inner child.
We all spend the rest of our lives banging on the windows of our own
nursery, forever shut out.
Forever looking for our own shadows.
No wonder we all get tired.
Jeff It's all right.
Kate (*to the audience*) Jeff's big moment.

But Jeff hasn't quite got the courage

Jeff It's the same in the motor trade. (*He rejoins the group*)
Anna Is it Max's you want to go back to?
Daniel Not likely.
Jenny It'd be Max's birthday and retirement a week on Friday.
If there was any stickability these days?

Daniel Max's all right, but he's always on about football.
Anna See, Grans, he wants to come home to you.
Jenny This is my home.
Kate It is not.
Anna Gramps *wants* you.
Jenny What he *wants* is someone to wash his towels.
　　I know him.
Anna And I think that is exactly what he wants.
Noon What?
Anna *Because* she knows him.
Noon That's … cool.
Anna I'm impressed myself.
　　So, while I'm on a roll, everyone…
Kate (*to the audience*) Anna's big speech.
Anna I'll tell you what me and Emma want.
　　I want to go to Cambridge, join the Footlights and take Frank up the
　　Backs on Saturdays in the summer and tell him I do love him after all.
Frank No.
Anna I might as well.
Frank You've got to mean it.
Anna I'll mean it, then.
　　I'll get him to kiss me in a punt with all my posh friends in striped
　　blazers eating strawberries and watching.
Frank No!
　　I don't want that.
Anna Diddums. What do you want, then?
Frank You.
Anna About time.
Frank But not like that.
Anna I'll keep saying I love you while we——
Frank With people looking.
Anna We'll have to shut our eyes, then.

And they are at peace

　　And meanwhile what *Emma* wants…

But Emma still won't speak

　　…is for you all to be normal.
　　So she can rebel like a proper teenager and then leave home and not find
　　her home's left her first.

Emma gets cuddled

Daniel I don't do nothing to them towels that isn't meant to be done to them.
Jenny You don't do *anything* to *those* towels.
Daniel Just what I were just saying.
Anna You should be saying you love her.
Daniel Who?
Anna Grans.
Daniel Why?
Anna It might get you some sleep tonight.
Daniel Saying I *love her*?
     She knows I love her.
     Why does she think we keep yelling?
     And what's she crying for now?
Jenny I'm crying for me. Look at my hands. Why am I old so soon?
Noon Hug her, Gramps.
Daniel I'm not *Gramps*.
Noon I feel you are to her.
Anna (*to Frank*) You crying too?
Frank I think so.
Kate (*to the audience*) And me.
     So at last.
     Everything *moves*.
     "Peace ho I bar confusion
     'Tis I must make conclusion
     Of these most strange events
     Here's eight that must take hands."
Noon (*leading all the hugs*) Yes!
     Let's all hug!
     Let's not be *alone*!
     Dare to share!
     Free the feminine!
     It's strong to be weak!
     Let's hold each other before we fall apart!

Kate gives Frank the key

Kate You might need it now?
Frank Thanks, Anna's mum.
     But I won't use it——
Kate We've not been through all this so…
Frank I was going to say I won't use it *often*?
Kate I wouldn't tell Anna.
Jenny (*to Daniel*) Next time somebody leaves it's *me* first.
     OK?

But by now everyone is hugging

> *As You Like It* or what?
> Except, of course, for me...
> And Max.

The Lights flicker

EPILOGUE

Late on a late June evening. And then even later

Kate (*on the phone*) You sound a bit funny.
> Max?...
> Jeff! Well, this is Kate. And I didn't like to ask you the other day at the therapy party but why didn't you come to see me in *When We Are Married*?...
> Then you should get yourself a nice little Peugeot two-oh-five because they are a little bit more reliable than you are.
> Put me on to Max, please...
> Tell him Rasputin can wait.

Pause

> Happy birthday...
> And Max? Thank you for coming to the play...
> Thanks. And you knock 'em in the aisles with old *Rasputin* as well then, eh?...

She puts the phone down. And it could be the end of the story

> (*To the audience*) A couple of days later, I'm looking out of the window.
> Going over my Clara Soppitt lines,
> Perfectly, like you do, after.
> And feeling incredibly sad cos it's over.
> But you're already starting thinking about who you'll be next time...
> And I see this rather natty green Espace outside.
> Well, Jeff's driving it.
> And it's full of everyone.
> And moments later I get a visitor.

Max enters

What do you want, Max?

Max My Cliff Richard album.

Kate Right.

Max Nice place.

She searches for the record

Actually, Jeff's just test-driving a Renault Espace RN/Helios he's got hold of.

Kate Nice motor?

Max A few electrical gremlins, and it retains the old poor pedal positioning.

Kate Into cars these days, are you?

Max Into all sorts.

Kate I've heard.

Max You'd be surprised.

Kate I was.

Pause

Thanks again for coming to see *When We Are Married*.

Max I still don't know how you know I did?

Kate Somebody was laughing in the wrong places.

Not one of my friends.

They bought tickets, of course, but they never turned up.

Max You were too young for Clara.

Kate I used to be.

I was cast as Nancy originally.

And once upon a time I was Ruby.

Max You were good.

Kate I forgot my lines.

Max I didn't notice.

Kate Twice.

Max I've done Rasputin for years.

But when I did it at my party I suddenly thought I've got it wrong. I can't be sure if it's Moscow or St Petersburg.

Kate We did Torquay twice too.

Max I didn't notice.

Kate Didn't Marx say *history* repeats itself too?

First as tragedy then as farce?

Max He did.

Kate We remember some things between us, then?

Max I think.

She gives him the Cliff record

Kate No love lost?
Max What's that then?
Kate A play we did.
     Here.
     Enjoy.

He takes the record

Max You enjoying college and work and all that?
Kate Yes, you enjoying early retirement and all that?
Max I will.
Kate Great.
Max Yes.

This might be their moment. But it isn't. She looks out of her window

     They've all got out of the Espace.
     Gramps and Grans.
     He's holding her hand across the road.
     Tugging her a bit close to that bus I'd say.
     Oh, and Frank and Anna. Well, what's he…?
     I suppose that's allowed now she loves him?
     Jeff and Noon.
     She's rubbing his shoulder, and he's pointing at a car.
     And little Emma—
     Not so little these days, is she?
     And they're all coming in.

Pause

Kate What's next, Max?
Max I'm a historian. I only know things when they've happened and don't
    matter any more. What about you?
Kate I'm an actor.
     Someone has to prompt me.

This could be their moment too. But the door bursts open

*The guests come in, ad-libbing loudly about the weather, the news, last
night's TV, Frank's mother's car, Cambridge, athlete's foot in old age,
and the possibilities of happiness*

The doorbell rings. This silences them

Kate goes out to let the visitor in

They wait wondering who it might be

Kate enters with Emma

       Emma got a bit delayed, didn't you?
Max What happened, Em?
Kate There was a young *man*.
       With a bike.

They all look at her. The lights are very bright

Emma He's only someone from school.
       He's not my boyfriend or anything.
       I don't fancy him. Really.
       He just stopped me and wanted to talk. I don't know him. He's in year
       eleven.
       He wants me to go to the end-of-term disco with him.
       He's called Julian.
       I might as well.
       Mightn't I?

The magical moment is held. Then Black-out and Cliff Richard singing The
Young Ones

The actors take their curtain

*And then a party quickly develops on stage and our final picture of them all
is them drinking, joking, and enjoying each other's company as they were at
the start of the evening*

The auditorium Lights go up

The stage Lights soon fade and they are gone

This final picture can be left out, of course

PRODUCTION NOTES

No Love Lost was one of the BT 1998 Biennial plays. That means that although it is a new play it has already been widely performed. There were also several workshops during its making, and innumerable phone calls, emails and letters. What follows are some tips I originally made for myself for when I direct the play next time, but other directors may find them useful too.

- Don't play it for laughs.
- Don't make the grandparents old, or anybody silly.
- Pretend it's real.
- Don't give it a "happy ending".
- Emma is a star, whether she plays accordion, saxophone, keyboard, trumpet or whatever. But she has to keep listening all the time or we forget she's there.
- Frank is better spiky.
- Noon shouldn't go over the top.
- Max and Kate are good people who do (some) bad things—but they can change.
- Anna is very bright.
- Jeff is good company.
- The going-backwards-then-going-forwards trick isn't a problem for audiences.
- In rehearsals it seems to help the performers sometimes to rehearse the play in "real" time. One company in the Biennial actually rehearsed the whole play like that (starting with the last scene in Act I and then going to the first in Act II, then Scene 7 in Act I, and so on) right up to their first tech.
- Max and Kate don't dominate the play like they might seem to on paper. Nor do they really have too much to learn—though every Max and every Kate grumbled about how hard it is to learn the "narrator" bits between scenes.
- The scene changes, marked in the script as lighting changes can be done in various ways. In some of the original productions the lights flickered, got brighter, turned into spotlights, had bits of music to accompany them, etc. What's really important is that there's no gap. As one scene clears, the next should have started. If Kate or Max have to walk somewhere to find a light to make a speech to walk out into the next scene, the play falls into pieces.
- The play can come in all shapes and sizes. The less scenery, the fewer props, the better. Anything that slows it up, like set or costume changes is dangerous.
- This script is deliberately unspecific (or unhelpful, if you like) about set,

costumes, and moves. It seems safe to ignore any stage directions that don't work (especially some of the "pauses").

• Every production and every performance is different. It's just as difficult every time, but in different ways. There are no answers, but we are all infinitely ingenious.

RR

FURNITURE AND PROPERTY LIST

Further dressing may be added at the director's discretion

ACT I

PROLOGUE

On stage: Drinks in glasses
Bottles
Flowers
Music system
Emma's musical instrument
Phone
Record collection
Torch

SCENE 1

On stage: As before

SCENE 2

Re-set: Glasses
Bottles

Strike: **Emma**'s musical instrument
Torch

Off stage: Bags, one containing medicines (**Jenny**)

SCENE 3

Strike: **Jenny**'s bags

Off stage: Tray of tea things including spoons (**Daniel**)

SCENE 4

Strike: Tea things

Off stage: Bananas (**Jenny**)
               Burger meal, musical instrument (**Emma**)

SCENE 5

Set: Bottle of Drambuie

Strike: Burger meal
               Bananas

SCENE 6

On stage: As before

Personal: **Frank:** key

SCENE 7

On stage: Beer
               Pen
               The *Observer*

Off stage: Huge bunch of flowers (**Frank**)

SCENE 8

On stage: As before

Personal: **Kate:** key

ACT II

SCENE 1

On stage: Tickets
          Glasses
          Phone

Off stage: Bottle of sherry (**Kate**)
           Cliff Richard record (**Frank**)

Personal: **Frank:** key, money

SCENE 2

Set: *When We Are Married* script

Off stage: The *Observer* (**Anna**)

SCENE 3

Strike: The *Observer*

Personal: **Frank:** key

SCENE 4

Set: Make-up
          Diary

SCENE 5

On stage: As before

Off stage: Instrument, teen magazine (**Emma**)
           Coat (**Kate**)

SCENE 6

On stage: As before

SCENE 7

Re-set: Bottle of gin
               Script

Off stage: Luggage (**Frank**)
               Wash bag (**Jenny**)

Personal: **Jenny:** toffee

SCENE 8

On stage: As before

Off stage: Can of beer (**Jeff**)
               Salad (**Jenny**)

Personal: **Kate:** key

EPILOGUE

Strike: Salad

LIGHTING PLOT

Property fittings required: nil
2 interiors

ACT I, PROLOGUE

To open: Fairly dim evening lighting, auditorium lights on

Cue 1   **Frank** turns lights off   (Page 1)
             Black-out

ACT I, SCENE 1

To open: Darkness

Cue 2   **Jeff** turns lights on   (Page 2)
             Bring up overall lighting

Cue 3   **Max**: "Hallo?"   (Page 7)
             Flicker lights

ACT I, SCENE 2

To open: Morning lighting

Cue 4   **Daniel**: "…I'm always here all the time now."   (Page 10)
             Flicker lights

ACT I, SCENE 3

To open: Morning lighting

Cue 5   **Max** turns to the audience   (Page 13)
             Flicker lights

ACT I, Scene 4

To open: Evening lighting

Cue 6   **Max**: "Emma. Talk?"   (Page 16)
               Flicker lights

ACT I, Scene 5

To open: Early evening lighting

Cue 7   **Daniel**: "I hate Drambuie."   (Page 21)
               Flicker lights

ACT I, Scene 6

To open: Afternoon lighting

Cue 8   **Noon** and **Max** go towards bedroom   (Page 28)
               Flicker lights

ACT I, Scene 7

To open: Morning lighting

Cue 9   **Anna** and **Frank** exit   (Page 35)
               Flicker lights

ACT I, Scene 8

To open: Late afternoon lighting

Cue 10   **Max** turns after **Emma**   (Page 40)
               Flicker lights

Cue 11   **Max**: "…in the deepest of winters and…"   (Page 40)
               Black-out

ACT II, SCENE 1

To open: Darkness

Cue 12 **Kate** turns lights on (Page 41)
  Bring up lights

Cue 13 **Kate** drinks (Page 44)
  Flicker lights

ACT II, SCENE 2

To open: Evening lighting

Cue 14 **Kate**: "…as you call them—Herbert Soppitt?" (Page 48)
  Flicker lights

ACT II, SCENE 3

To open: Morning lighting

Cue 15 Phone rings (Page 51)
  Flicker lights

ACT II, SCENE 4

To open: Evening lighting

Cue 16 **Emma** plays, then stops (Page 52)
  Flicker lights

ACT II, SCENE 5

To open: Overall general lighting

Cue 17 **Jenny** and **Emma** exit (Page 54)
  Flicker lights

Cue 18   **Kate**: "I do not enter at once…"   (Page 54)
               Flicker lights

ACT II, SCENE 6

To open: Dim morning lighting

Cue 19   **Kate** and **Jeff** go to bed   (Page 60)
               Flicker lights

ACT II, SCENE 7

To open: Morning lighting

Cue 20   **Anna**: "Oh an' how long…"   (Page 66)
               Flicker lights

Cue 21   **Kate**: "The Sunday after the show."   (Page 66)
               Flicker lights

ACT II, SCENE 8

To open: Afternoon lighting

Cue 22   **Jenny**: "And Max."   (Page 77)
               Flicker lights

ACT II, EPILOGUE

To open: Late evening lighting

Cue 23   **All** look at **Emma**   (Page 80)
               Bright lighting; after a pause, black-out

Cue 24   **Emma**: "Mightn't I?"   (Page 80)
               After a pause, black-out, then lights up for the curtain call

Cue 25   Party develops   (Page 80)
               Bring up auditorium lights; begin to fade stage lights down

EFFECTS PLOT

Cue 1   To open   (Page 1)
Party music

Cue 2   **Anna** turns music off   (Page 1)
Cut music

Cue 3   **Max**: "Rasputin!"   (Page 7)
Phone rings

Cue 4   Black-out   (Page 40)
Music: Cliff Richard's Bachelor Boy

Cue 5   **Kate** begins to drink   (Page 41)
Doorbell rings

Cue 6   **Kate**: "…in J B Priestley's *When We Are——*"   (Page 41)
Doorbell rings

Cue 7   **Kate**: "But——"   (Page 45)
Phone rings, doorbell rings

Cue 8   **Kate**: "…Marx said but Max said——"   (Page 51)
Phone rings

Cue 9   **Kate**: "…in early March, exit Kate E——"   (Page 53)
Doorbell rings forcefully

Cue 10   **Kate**: "The door is open—Mother."   (Page 53)
Doorbell rings

Cue 11   **Kate**: "…since she got her new teeth."   (Page 53)
Doorbell rings

Cue 12   To open Act II, Scene 7   (Page 60)
Doorbell rings, after a pause rings again

| *Cue* 13 | **All** come in and chat | (Page 79) |
| | *Doorbell rings* | |

| *Cue* 14 | **Emma**: "Mightn't I?" | (Page 80) |
| | *After a pause, music: Cliff Richard's* The Young Ones | |